TARIKA'S MEDITATIONS ON THE FRIDGE: FREEDOM FROM DIETING BY MAINTAINING YOUR WEIGHT MINDFULLY

BY
TARIKA LOVEGARDEN

Meditations on the Fridge: Freedom from Dieting by Maintaining Your Weight Mindfully
By Tarika Lovegarden

ISBN Number: 978-0-692-67482-6
Published by Mindful Matters Publishing, LLC.
www.MeditationsOnTheFridge.com

AUTHOR'S NOTE

This book contains the opinions and ideas of its author. It is intended to provide helpful and informative material on the subject it addresses. It is sold with the understanding that the author/publisher are not engaged in rendering medical, psychological, health or any other kind of personal professional advice or services in the book. It is not meant to contradict, disregard, or interfere with advice or care from any such professionals.

SPECIAL NOTE TO READERS WITH MEDICAL CONDITIONS RELATED TO OVER OR UNDER EATING

Eating disorders are a potentially life-threatening illness and any program to improve healthy eating practices should include the advice and direction of a Medical Doctor. The author and publisher of this book do not make any medical claims in this book and it should be very clear that while the author has succeeded in applying the knowledge in this book to overcome her food cravings that her case is not typical and that the reader may not be able to achieve the same results. Please consult a medical professional if you have unhealthy eating behaviors.

In some instances, names of individuals and entities have been changed to protect their privacy.

What the experts are saying about *Meditations on the Fridge* by Tarika Lovegarden

"Information is important but not usually sufficient to motivate people to make lasting changes in what they eat and how they live. More effective is to address the underlying feelings that underlie our behaviors. By working at that level, Tarika empowers people to make lifestyle choices that are life-enhancing rather than self-destructive."

Dean Ornish, M.D.
Founder & President, Preventive Medicine Research Institute
Clinical Professor of Medicine, University of California, San Francisco
Author, Eat More, Weigh Less and The Spectrum

———————

"Writing on such a loaded topic as food and how to best to enjoy it, is not necessarily an easy ride. However, Ms. Lovegarden has overcome many hurdles and faced down her demons to create this loving, informative and inspirational book. If you eat, read it! And if you don't eat, read it, anyway. It is a powerful meditation on how to nourish ourselves in a conscious and transcendent manner."

Deva Premal and Miten

———————

"Meditations on the Fridge is Tarika's gift to the World. Finally she addresses a mindful way to managing your weight based upon the time honored, heart-center meditations. No more feeling bad about yourself. Let Tarika Lovegarden be your guide for this journey of appreciation of where you are right now and help you overcome the acute food cravings that affect some of us in painful ways. Let Tarika shine her loving wisdom to support you and give you strength."

Marci Shimoff

*Dedicated to those who
want to learn to love their
bodies, and enjoy foods that
are right for them, so that
they can maintain a
comfortable weight,
naturally.*

Table of Contents

Introduction

Welcome. It is with deep love and compassion for your suffering- big or small, continual or occasional, that I share this healing process with you. Tarika's Meditations" empower you to make healthy choices in every day and challenging food situations, giving you freedom from unhealthy habits and addictive eating. They connect you to your innate wisdom, so that you can feel what your body needs, and respond accordingly.

I'll begin by sharing my story. As you read my struggles with food, self-worth, and how my relationships with men affected my weight, let your own story surface so that it can heal and be released. It may bring up memories from childhood, or later in life, when you ate to meet challenges, needs, or to try and change how you feel. You may discover that some of those innocent strategies have become destructive patterns, even though your life circumstances may have changed. Becoming more aware of your triggers and habits is the first step to changing them.

You may find similarities, or your food issues may be very different to mine. Your issues may stem from a lack of fulfillment in your intimate relationships, or you may be satisfied with your partner, and have entirely different issues that trigger your unhealthy choices. You may have weight to lose, or you might be skinny, but feel ashamed and deprived because you don't allow yourself to eat much. You may suffer from anorexia or bulimia. You might fluctuate like I have, and suffer more than someone who weighs more than you. Or you might have a lot of weight to lose, and feel tremendous pressure from the threat of serious health consequences if you don't lose weight.

The beauty about this process is that it will work for you regardless of how much you weigh, your obsessions or imbalances with food, or the deeper issues that drive your food choices. We suffer because we're not connected to our deeper nature- our soul, regardless of the motives and manifestations of our unhealthy habits. These meditations transform your eating habits, and consequently your body, by connecting you with your inner strengths and true nature. You have everything you need to be healthy, happy and fulfilled.

As you read my story I hope that you feel understood, less ashamed, and that you recognize there's nothing wrong with you for overeating. You're not damaged. You are lovable, even though your body may not be where you want it to be right now. I'm here to help you become balanced, healthier, more beautiful, more confident, relaxed with food, and to find a weight that's comfortable and easy to maintain.

This isn't about being skinny, how much you weigh, or your shape and size. I hope that your body transforms in the ways you want it to, and that this process enables you to maintain a comfortable weight that makes you feel beautiful, without worrying about what you eat. Weight loss usually follows once you settle into a healthy, satisfying rhythm of eating.

As you understand your issues more deeply, and recognize how your eating habits originated, you'll likely feel compassion for yourself. Instead of criticizing yourself for the unhealthy ways you learned to cope, you can use your innate wisdom to look for fulfilling ways to nurture and care for yourself. These meditations connect you with your true power, so that you can respond to your emotional needs, and life circumstances intelligently, and intuitively.

These meditations give you space from the impulses of cravings, so that instead of falling slave to your desires, or mustering willpower to resist them, you can make empowering choices. As you transcend the duality of control and indulgence– dieting and "cheating", you discover balanced, nourishing ways of eating.

I've never felt understood by trainers who say things like, "Stop eating Chocolate." Or, "You must be eating too much Bread, you look puffy." Sadly, I received both those comments from excellent trainers who meant well, but didn't have a clue about the challenges we face, or more important, how to help a compulsive eater like me.

I nearly burst into tears and ran out of the Gym. I hadn't eaten Bread in months or Chocolate in weeks, but started thinking about Chocolate on my way home. It took all of my courage to work out after bingeing, and their comments only made me want to hide and eat.

I won't judge you no matter what you're eating, or tell you to eliminate anything you're not ready to let go of. I invite you to build upon your strengths, empowering you to find nourishing foods to satisfy your cravings, rather than depriving yourself of your favorite foods. I'm here to support and guide you every step of the way, at your own pace. I may lovingly challenge you at times, but I won't pressure you to make commitments you can't keep. I know how heartbreaking it is when you're trying as hard as you can to eat healthily, and then unconscious habits take over in spite of your resolve.

I created this program when my patterns of dieting and bingeing, the endless battle to control my weight, stopped working. I realized that every diet led me to binge; so dieting anymore would be futile, and yet I refused to become obese. After feeling defeated time and time again I gave up trying, but I still wasn't at peace. I burned out on exercise after years of pushing myself to extremes in order to burn off my nightly binges, yet I still needed to move my body. I scheduled my life around eating, yet I was terrified of gaining weight. It was an excruciating dilemma, with which you can probably identify.

I was determined to find peace and enjoy my body. I decided to turn my biggest suffering into an opportunity for spiritual growth. I realized meditation was the only way I would heal. Not knowing where else to turn, I humbly asked my parents for help.

Even though Leela (my mother) and Prasad (my father) separated when I was three years old, they've worked together ever since. When Prasad got remarried to Alvina, over 25 years ago, the three of them began working together.

They're internationally renowned meditation teachers. They've designed countless mindfulness based therapeutic processes to free people of their suffering, while training therapists and leaders, in spiritual communities for over 40 years.

They have an extraordinary, reverential relationship. Their united gifts have transformed countless lives through meditation. I consider them to be the most powerful healers on the planet; each uniquely talented, yet complementary.

They've trained me to teach meditation since I was a child. These meditations were created from my receptivity and connection to that which is bigger than me, and from my three parents' mentoring and support. Our combined talents and experience, and our devotion to divine awakening, are the foundation of this work. My boundless creativity, and ability to channel these transformative processes, enabled me to ground profound states of consciousness, into practical tools to help you make healthy food choices. Since I feel like I channeled this work, and to this day I need to be mindful of what I eat, I'm a disciple of my own teaching. I practice these meditations regularly, and attentively review the golden nuggets of truth herein, especially when I fall into unhealthy habits.

I don't think there's a "right" way to heal, or way of eating that works for everyone. I help you discover what works for you, while teaching you to respond to your needs and ever-changing environment.

Some of my clients benefit from calorie counting, food plans, and raw food cleanses, when they're connected to their sources of self-care and body wisdom. They can be excellent tools to bring you into balance, and become attuned to your body. Do whatever works.

This process is designed to free you from dieting. When you're connected to your deeper nature, you can use numerous methods as a bridge to freedom. These meditations transform your understanding of dietary approaches, so that what may have seemed like food prison, can become a guardian angel of loving light. Many of you will transform simply by connecting with your body wisdom, as I'll be guiding you throughout this process, and you won't need dietary structure from outside.

Even though I'm a nutritionist, and recommend basic nutritional principles like eating whole foods in appropriate quantities, staying hydrated, getting enough sleep, and finding the right balance of macronutrients for your biochemical individuality, I've devoted this book to helping you connect with your own wisdom. I believe your wisdom is the key to having what you want. As you learn to listen to your body, you'll lose, and/or maintain your weight, by enjoying food, rather than depriving yourself.

You've probably begun to recognize your issues run deeper than any diet or exercise program can address. Changing what you eat usually works for a while, as long as you're able to stick to it, but it doesn't transform the reasons that drive you to overeat.

Meditation connects you with your deeper nature– your soul, which is often what we're attempting to get from food. We eat as a way to connect with ourselves. We eat to avoid uncomfortable feelings, stimulate pleasurable ones, and to try and fulfill unmet needs. We eat out of habit, simply because we've eaten that way for years. We eat because of others, advertisements, or cultural influences. The reasons we eat are endless, and always changing.

These meditations enable you to identify your triggers and patterns, while connecting with yourself at a level so intimately satisfying; you'll no longer be compelled to reach for food instead.

There are many incredible benefits to meditation, like blissful states of peace, intuitive wisdom and power, that you'll likely experience throughout this program. More important, I'll be teaching you how meditation heals your relationship with food.

On an intuitive level you probably know what to eat, but information can be confusing. One diet book tells you to eat your biggest meal at breakfast and another tells you to only eat fruit until noon. This kind of conflicting information can prevent you from connecting with, and trusting your own wisdom, which is what will inevitably heal you. Your body will tell you what it needs, if you pay attention. Many of these meditations are a practice in receiving your bodies' messages, while others help you release the emotions and mindsets that block you from following them.

Perhaps you feel you can't trust yourself with food, or that at times your appetite is insatiable. You may have tried restricting "fattening" foods like Sugar, fried foods, carbs, alcohol, and/or fats. As you connect with your body you'll feel more satisfied with less food, and you'll discover how much of your festive favorites you can enjoy without gaining weight. If you're reading this book I'm assuming you're seeking a long-term solution. Freedom. Love. Fulfillment.

Who wants to feel deprived, left out at social gatherings, and hungry all the time? Your body's survival mechanisms, which are stronger than willpower, will eventually kick in and make you eat. When you discover the nourishing foods, ideal quantities, and settle into a rhythm of eating that's right for you, your cravings will disappear, and your weight will stabilize.

We all have the strengths necessary to make healthy food choices. Some are simply more developed than others. These meditations illuminate and water your innate qualities, so they flower and become available to you. Some of your strengths may be in seed form, while others are in full bloom. Think of me as a gardener tending to, nurturing, and watering the fertile ground of your inner potential. As I guide you into meditation, caring for yourself and eating healthily will come naturally. As your energy is freed from battling temptations and worrying about your weight, your life will blossom in ways you can't imagine.

Remember, you're not alone. Like many others, you can use the power of meditation, and the grace of your heart to heal these issues, so that you have the body and life you truly desire.

How To Use This Book

I recommend reading this book in its entirety, so that you can deeply receive these treasures of becoming mindful with food. If you like, you can mark the sections you resonate with and revisit them to experiment with the meditations that appeal to you.

Chapters 5 and after focus on a specific food situations, like grocery shopping, cooking, eating, social situations, cravings, and stopping when your body's had enough. If you can master each of these situations by making healthy, satisfying choices consistently, you'll likely have the body and life you desire. If you go overboard every time you eat out for example, it can easily undermine your efforts, even if you make excellent choices in all the other food situations.

It's usually best to practice making healthy choices in the simplest situations first. I've given them in the order that works well for most people, but if you feel drawn to start with a specific situation, go for it.

It was easiest for me to make healthy choices at the grocery store. I made decisions in a split second, whereas at home it was almost impossible for me to resist eating the foods that triggered my compulsion. Teaching myself how to cook was the next situation I tackled, which was much easier than portion control.

Building your healthy-choice-muscle in the situations that are easiest for you will give you the strength and momentum to master your challenges. Some of you may only have one or two downfalls, if that's the case focus on the chapters that address your weaknesses. If you've struggled long-term, you'll likely need to bring mastery to several, if not all, of the food situations to transform your body and life.

You may surprise yourself when you recognize how your mindless eating habits take over in situations where you thought you made excellent choices.

Before I wrote this book I thought my biggest challenge was sneak eating, and that I made reasonable choices in social situations until I became more aware. I also realized that many of my binges began with my choices at the grocery store, and that my cravings only disappeared after I stopped eating refined, processed foods.

Each chapter contains meditations I've practiced and perfected for years on myself, and clients to help you master the unique challenges each food situation presents. I've given you shortened versions and supportive practices that accompany Tarika's Meditations on the Fridge audio meditation series to ensure your success. This book is especially useful if you'd like to understand the process of becoming mindful.

Each chapter corresponds with one of my 15-20 min recorded meditations, which guides you through the process of making healthy food choices in the food situation at hand. They're like mental rehearsals, addressing common challenges, while connecting you with your inner strengths, so that you can be centered and make empowering choices, instead of falling into mindless habits.

You'll still need to practice the techniques in real-life situations, like when you're craving popcorn at the theatre, or ordering food in social situations. As you practice making healthy choices it will become easier and easier.

You can listen to them in any order, even as you continue reading. Or you can wait until you've read the whole book to listen to them. It takes practice and patience, but I promise you the results are well worth it. Imagine what it would be like to enjoy food and not worry about your weight, because you naturally make satisfying choices, in any situation.

The meditative practices throughout the book and audio meditations are packed with effective techniques, so I highly recommend taking advantage of both by reading, listening, and then practicing making healthy choices as much as you can. Reading through the meditative practices, even if you do not take the time to practice them in that moment will likely help you, and enhance the efficacy of the recorded meditations. In other words, this book, and the Tarika's Meditations on the Fridge audio meditation series go hand in hand. Each chapter is named after its corresponding audio meditation. You can purchase them from my website: www.TarikaLovegarden.com and sign up to receive free sample meditations and to be alerted of promotional savings on my latest meditation program releases.

When you listen to my meditations, simply sit, or lie back, relax, and I will guide you through your personal journey of transformation.

I recommend keeping a food journal, or making notes throughout this process to record your insights, triggers, and subsequent food choices. Writing about what you eat, and how your body responds to different foods and quantities, gives you valuable information.

Meditations on the Fridge by Tarika Lovegarden

Acknowledgements

There have been so many heart-wrenching challenges in which I lost hope and belief in myself. Thankfully there was always someone who saw my potential and stood by me when I desperately wanted to give up. Their belief in me carried me through years of hard work, as I developed these meditations without any apparent reward. I felt driven to fulfill my destiny.

Prasad stood by me through the "darkest night of my soul", which lasted several years as I purified karmic patterns, and moved through debilitating fears of success. I couldn't have blossomed without his boundless patience, unconditional love, and belief in me. He spent hours every week on the phone with me, year after year, listening to me sob as I lost hope. He taught me how to become conscious, transform my suffering, and to help others do the same. He transmitted the essence of these powerful processes, sharing his approach to meditation– the flowering of Leela, Alvina, and his life's work.

Antonio helped me write this book, even though I could barely write an email when we first met. I couldn't even read or write a single word of English (and that's my native tongue) until I was eleven years old! When he asked me what I did I choked back tears as I described my vision. He saw something in me, and generously devoted hours of his time, for years, to help me deliver this work. He's a hero and an angel. You wouldn't be reading this without him.

22

Leela has given to me unconditionally in so many ways, on so many levels. She helped me connect with my intuition– a deep knowing that's enabled me to perceive life, others, and myself with clarity and authenticity. I often communicate with Leela without words. I can feel it when we understand each other. She continually works on realms that most people can't even cognize. In addition to her phenomenal intuitive power, her heart and emotional intelligence are equally as strong. She's nurtured those same strengths in me. I feel eternally grateful to her as my mother, friend, mentor, and spiritual teacher. She's an extraordinary healer, with a huge capacity for love. Even when she wasn't with me as a child I felt her love across oceans. In one word, she is love.

Alvina has an incredible depth of sensitivity and intuitive perception. She can sense what a person is struggling with, or what's causing their suffering, and how to help them.

Her wide range of experience in intimate relating that has led to astonishing intelligence has been miraculously healing. She's helped me in ways my parents weren't able to. She helped me break through stubborn, stuck places when I felt victimized by life– paralyzed by hopelessness as I was convinced I would never become free of compulsive eating. She helped me feel and transform painful emotions from the disappointments I suffered over men. She brought me back to my center when my insurmountable expectations and demands made it impossible for a man to fulfill me. I learned to find love within, so that I was able to receive what a man had to give.

23

I doubt I would have completed this book without Marga, my Italian translator, friend, and wise-woman sister. She too saw my gifts and created the opportunities for me to deliver this work in Italy, which is where it began.

Chapter One

My Story: A Woman Trapped in a Chubby Teenager's Body

My extraordinary, yet challenging life began in San Francisco in 1979. I feel blessed to have been immersed in meditation since I was in my mother's womb.

When I was three years old, we moved to a spiritual community in Oregon, and my parents separated as they pursued their spiritual awakening. The commune was a self-sufficient town of 7,000 residents, built on 64,000 acres of agricultural land.

There was a lake, several restaurants, cafes, and a mall. We had our own fire and police departments, a hospital, and public transportation. To me, it seemed like paradise. I felt I belonged to a huge "family" of seekers of truth, as even at that age I was in touch with my longing to awaken.

I lived in a dormitory with about fifteen kids, and saw each of my parents just once a week. Although, as an adult, I understand their choices, as a three-year-old I felt neglected.

I was quick to adapt to new environments and make new friends, so that on the surface, all seemed well. But deep down, I unconsciously interpreted their neglect as proof I was unlovable. If they really cared about me, I thought, they wouldn't have left me. Now I know my parents loved me, and, like the rest of us, they were riveted by the immense opportunity our spiritual teacher had created for us.

However, all week I yearned to be with them. To deal with my feelings of insecurity and need for attention, I ate to comfort myself. Whenever I got the chance, I'd run through the bakery's kitchen and grab as many freshly baked Chocolate chip cookies as I could, frantically gobbling them down, while hiding some in my pockets for later. At meals I mostly ate white Bread with margarine, cinnamon and white Sugar.

Sometimes my dad would take me out to lunch and I'd enjoy a plate of nachos– one of my childhood favorites. I'd eagerly soak up every drop of attention, feeling special for a day, until I had to go back to the dormitory.

I remember spending evenings with my mother, cuddling up with her in bed. Even though she and my father mutually decided to separate, I think a part of her suffered emotionally.

When we moved to the community my parents were encouraged to explore their sexuality, so they separated to fulfill their wedding vows of freedom. They had promised to support each other's divine awakening above all else, and that's precisely what they've done to this day. I think their deep love for each other was primarily a soul connection rather than romantic love.

I don't know the cause of her pain. It may have been residual attachment from the dissolution of her relationship with my dad, or had to do with other men she was dating, or maybe it was just her huge heart channeling the pain of humanity. Whatever the cause, I remember wrapping my little arms around her, wishing I could take away her pain. I remember wondering why she was always on a diet; watching her eat tofu and brown rice for days.

Many of our eating habits develop in childhood, and children soak up their parents' behaviors like sponges. I see myself in my mother every time we eat together.

Not only have I felt ancient since the day I can remember; I was also in touch with my power. Even at four years old I spoke to the most powerful grown-ups in charge of the commune as equals—people who terrified other grown-ups.

My mother tells a story about me challenging, Rachael, one of the most powerful bosses in our community. Rachael was giving orders on how she wanted things changed in our kindergarten. I stood in front of her with my little hands on my hips, looking straight into her eyes, and wouldn't move. Eventually Rachael stopped shouting and looked back at me. I discussed the situation with her as an equal, and apparently she considered my suggestions. Our caretakers said it looked as though my strength matched hers.

At the same time, unfortunately, I never got to be a child. I grew up quickly and became self-sufficient in order to survive, but lacked the stable support every child craves. Despite my independence, there were probably just as many times I felt insecure, although I tried not to show it by acting tough. I soothed and nursed those feelings with food.

I was five years old when we left Oregon and for years after that I experienced no stability, being left behind unexpectedly, or tagging along with my parents as they traveled, teaching meditation.

27

Soon after that I got shipped to a summer camp in Spain and I didn't even know who would pick me up at the airport. A welcoming family, also spiritual seekers, greeted me, but all I remember of the next six months is crying through long siestas with a pillow over my head, wishing I could disappear and die. I don't remember eating anything at all.

Switching between under eating and overeating is a common pattern. Some of us spend years on one side, totally oblivious of the other side buried deep within our subconscious. I've often forgotten I had a problem with food, because there have been years at a time when I effortlessly maintained a slender figure, until my emotional needs were no longer being met and my problems with food resurfaced.

After summer camp in Spain I flew to Florida. I spent six months in first grade living with my grandmother, Nana, who showed me her love by letting me have as much candy as I wanted, so I went back to overeating.

After that, I tagged along with my parents for several months while they led meditation workshops throughout Western Europe, and later India and Japan. I spent long days alone feeling neglected, while they taught from morning until night. Within that time a spiritually based international boarding school opened in Devon, England. Terrified yet again by the insecurity of not knowing what I'd find there, I reluctantly boarded a plane to England, where I stayed through high school.

It was nestled in the deep Devonshire countryside on approximately one hundred acres of land, surrounded by forests and fields. The nearest town, Chawleigh was a ten-minute walk. It had a pub, sweet shop, petrol pump, and a church.

Growing up there was one of my life's greatest blessings, but at first I felt as though I was amongst strangers. It was heartbreaking to be separated from my parents yet again. I was starting to get used to being alone, having been uprooted so many times, but my independence didn't lessen the pain.

I became domineering in order to protect myself from feeling vulnerable. My wounds of abandonment made me highly sensitive, and as a result I closed part of my heart. I only let people in to a certain degree, so that I still felt safe and in control. The benefits of opening my heart to the nourishing connections I longed for didn't seem worth the risk of being left alone, yet again.

I ate to soothe my pain. I couldn't trust anyone to be there for me, so I didn't expose myself to more abandonment by letting myself need anyone. I tried to fill my need for attention with food. Food gave me a sense of security and relief. Food was the only thing I could rely on, like a loyal friend. Food never abandoned me.

I ate at every opportunity. Even though we had three meals a day plus snacks of toast, biscuits, and fruit in the afternoon and evening, I snacked between snacks, so I was hardly hungry at meals. Candy was, of course, my favorite, but Bread, cereal, and cookies were also satisfying. Taking care of myself and eating healthily at boarding school was out of the question, at least in my mind. I didn't have any good role models, or proper supervision, and because it was a vegetarian school they mostly served pasta, or cheese toast with baked beans.

Nana continued to shower me with love in the form of care packages from Florida: Reese's Peanut Butter Cups, Snickers bars, candy corn at Halloween; each delivery was a delicious bounty of sweets, sweets, and more sweets! With no supervision I could eat an entire bag of candy in one sitting. Fulfilling my cravings soothed and satisfied me, even though I sometimes ate until I felt sick.

As well as soothing myself, I used food to connect with others. I'd gather my friends at school and organize trips to eat cake at local tearooms. In the Devonshire towns, we'd eat large scones with huge dollops of clotted cream with homemade strawberry jam. I'd be in pain for hours afterward, feeling an indigestible rock in my stomach. I gained weight with each unhealthy mouthful. I was getting fatter, and increasingly unhappy with my shape and size. I began to experience the connection between unhealthy eating, indigestion, and weight gain—the downsides of food's comforts.

I was maturing early, too, and boys teased me about my curvaceous figure, which made things worse. I was uncomfortable and ashamed. At eleven years old I felt like I was trapped in a woman's body, with large breasts and hips, while my friends were skinny and undeveloped.

I recognize now that I've always had a strong effect on men. But most boys, or men for that matter, didn't know how to handle me even when I was barely a teenager. I didn't know how to handle myself! I'd run up to my favorite boys and play with them until they were painfully turned on. Then I'd run away as they gave chase in a hot frenzy, to playfully yet forcefully pin me down. I got excited and slightly afraid, but I loved it. It was innocent and fun. My oozing sexuality excited them. It didn't seem to matter that I wasn't skinny. I was never really fat either, just a little chubby. Since then, I've come to realize that most men aren't nearly as critical as we are about ourselves, and each other. And perhaps many men don't even prefer skinny women, or they're just swayed by society's current aesthetic.

I got my period that year, too, and started seeing a handsome, loyal sixteen-year-old. He was a fantastic guy who loved me deeply. After a few years together, I fell in love with another guy. The very brief triangle—thank God it was end of term—was painful for everyone. Even though it was only teenage love, I swore I'd never do it again, and I never have. After my boyfriend and my new love left, I was more interested in graduating a year early than finding a new boyfriend. I couldn't wait to take on new adventures. At the time, I was happy and focused on the future. As at all such times, food wasn't really an issue, even though I always wanted to be skinnier.

At fifteen, I finished high school a year early and flew to a spiritual community in Pune, India. My parents had been based there since we left Oregon and I had spent most my vacations there, so it seemed like the natural place to go next. Even though they moved back to America only months after I arrived, I wanted to stay with my friends in India.

The community was based in what seemed like an oasis in the middle of an overpopulated, polluted Indian city. There were huge luscious tropical gardens, a large luxurious swimming pool, a sauna, Jacuzzis, tennis courts and various sports facilities, cafes, bars, and restaurants. We had an enormous marble meditation hall with mosquito netting that seated thousands from around the world. People would come to meditate, participate in workshops, hang out, or take part in the work-as-meditation program. Some would come for a few weeks, and for many, like myself, it was our home year round.

I lived with my friend Bettina, a German twenty-five-year-old, in a two-bedroom apartment five minutes from the commune by scooter. I learned to drive quickly, navigating through the dangerous Indian traffic without any rules or traffic lights, dodging holy herds of cows. They clearly had the right-of-way. We had to intuitively bully our way through, and the horn was our best weapon, by far.

Our place was comfortable and clean– a palace for India. I had a queen-sized mattress on the floor with some bamboo shelving in the corner, and my own bathroom. Many of our friends had to walk outside to use communal bathrooms.

We mostly hung out in the living room or with the community, and I often tagged along with her when she went on dates. We were inseparable.

Bettina was extremely sensual. She'd boast loudly that she always had "the most beautiful boyfriends." I admit most of them were gorgeous, fun, juicy men. At fifteen, I looked up to her as a mentor, older sister, and trusted friend. She felt like family. She became my legal guardian when my parents moved back to America. As a teenager I was happy to be on my own with so much freedom. They left me with plenty of cash and my dad's designer silk bedding.

Even though my first love had been incredibly nourishing, I still felt unworthy and ashamed of my body. I was ready to explore my sexuality and blissfully surrender to men. Sadly, I felt I needed to be skinny in order to do that, and was fed up with perceiving myself as fat. I compared myself and envied one friend in particular, Sarah, for her beauty and power over men. I desperately wanted to be as attractive. I wanted her long blonde hair, big blue eyes with long lashes, slender figure, perky breasts, and perfect bubble butt.

One day I was sitting with her near the pool on a swing in the cappuccino bar. I felt bad that I couldn't open to her when she genuinely wanted to connect. I told her how much I envied her. She unnecessarily apologized and threw her arms around me, trying to reassure me of my beauty. I received her love as I recognized I couldn't blame her for being beautiful. However, from then on my desire to become skinny became stronger than hunger.

I stopped eating and became anorexic. I ignored my hunger and made food my enemy. I feared food and felt uncomfortable eating, because I was convinced that everything I ate would make me fat.

I was determined to lose weight, so I became very strict with myself. I would only allow myself a cup of chai for breakfast. If I got hungry I'd snack on cough drops, chewable vitamin C, and water until lunch. Lunch was usually a small piece of papaya or an apple. Dinner was an apple with another cup of tea. When I was really starving, I'd allow myself one slice of whole wheat Bread with a banana, but I'd feel guilty for "overeating."

My fear of food was affecting my social life. I structured my day to avoid eating, or lied, saying I had already eaten at restaurants and parties. I still felt fat, ashamed of my body, and no more beautiful than when I was eating. I got so used to the high of feeling empty that I wasn't even interested in food. I didn't find pleasure in eating anymore, so hunger became the norm; physiological impacts joined my concerns about how my body looked.

I became ashamed to eat in front of others. I occasionally ate a piece of toast with Bettina, or shared a plate of food with my dear friend Coralie. I felt okay sharing their food, as they both expressed motherly care towards me, but I didn't have the confidence to select my own. Or perhaps I feared that if I focused on food, or made a habit of eating I'd get fat again.

No matter how much weight I lost—and by that time I was too skinny—all I saw was fat. Every time I looked in the mirror, I hated what I saw. My hips and thighs looked enormous to me. I had this insane idea, as anorexics often do, that if I ate anything at all, people would think I was a pig. I didn't deserve to eat.

I felt unattractive, no matter how thin I became. I continued to starve myself, thinking that if I got even skinnier I might become lovable. Unfortunately, I was blind to my beauty.

After a few months of hanging out with Bettina, I met Gustave, a French bodywork instructor, and fell in love. He'd massage me for hours, caressing and admiring the body I despised. His sensuous, soothing touch was profoundly healing. We'd lay together in his tree-house bungalow for hours with the warm tropical breeze delicately dancing on our skin. We'd make love, eat papaya, make love, eat more papaya, and then we'd drink screwdrivers while he prepared dinner. For about five months, it was heavenly–a remarkable initiation into womanhood. I trusted him enough to open my heart.

I ate a bit of fruit during the day, and only picked at the healthy meals he prepared, so I lost even more weight, and without much food I didn't need much to feel tipsy. I was innocent and burgeoning; it was one of the most beautiful phases of my life physically. My body has been beautiful in different ways since then, but sadly, I never felt beautiful enough.

When he left me for an older woman, after I had developed a puerile crush on his best friend, I decided to go back to America to live with my parents in Sedona, Arizona. It was the first time I spent any length of time with them since being separated from them at three years old. I thoroughly enjoyed their attention, like an innocent, happy child.

That was the only time in my life I let myself be a child. I've always called my parents by name. Even though they've always been my teachers, they treated me as an equal.

Soon after I arrived in Sedona, I met Michael. We were in a nurturing relationship for about a year and a half. I still wasn't interested in food, so I nibbled on apples while I watched him eat hamburgers. One night he came over and we were about to make love, when my body said no! I was surprised, because I thought I still loved him. Then it happened a few more times, and I couldn't ignore it. We had made love every day, and then for some reason, from one day to the next it was over. I left him, but he moved on more quickly, and found a new girlfriend. I isolated myself and ate rice cakes instead.

They were fat free. I was still terrified of gaining weight, but I couldn't ignore my hunger any longer. I started to eat whole packets of plain rice cakes and big bowls of air-popped popcorn to comfort myself. I'd sneak into my room each night, and soon I was devouring two packets of rice cakes in a row. I didn't find them very satisfying, so I just kept eating. I started to develop a compulsive eating disorder. I tried to soothe my pain with each mouthful. I literally sobbed between bites, crying and eating for hours, night after night, for almost a year. No matter how many packets of rice cakes I ate, I still felt empty inside.

I was the one who ended the relationship, and yet deep down I was terrified of being abandoned. I desperately wanted to be with a man again. As I sat alone in my room each night, I'd switch back and forth between fantasizing about the man of my dreams, and feeling hopeless and unlovable.

Whenever a man gave me a crumb of attention, I'd want to eat the whole cake. Sometimes just a look or a compliment got me fantasizing about how many children we'd have. For a while I was infatuated with a guy who gave me attention, but wasn't serious about me. I was in love with a fantasy of what I wanted him to be. I spent months mulling over everything he said, brooding over whether he loved me or not. Now I see the absurdity of it, but at the time it was heartbreaking.

After about a year of eating rice cakes I lost control and started pigging out on cake. I was working as a dessert chef at The Sage, a beautiful vegetarian buffet-style restaurant. It's ironic that I had such a talent for creating heavenly sweets when food was such torment for me. Sometimes I'd eat three desserts in a row, with huge dollops of whipped cream. I was eating the same way I had eaten in school, when I was gorging on scones and clotted cream.

A couple times my cravings were so strong I snuck out after everyone was asleep and drove to Safeway. I'd park on a quiet, dark street and frantically gorge myself, after having starved all day. I'd devour ice cream bars, bags of chips, or Chocolate chip cookies, while swallowing huge lumps of guilt and shame. I'd buy something salty and sweet to satisfy my cravings.

The next day I'd punish myself by not eating. Sometimes I would take herbal laxatives or start a "cleanse", but would end up quitting—which I saw as failing—when I got hungry. I only knew extremes. Either I was pigging out on fattening foods, compulsively eating fat-free foods, or sipping water and herbal teas, without much in between. It became a cycle.

Even though I starved myself each day, my night-time binges were steadily making me gain weight. Once again, I began to hate myself. I felt so ashamed that I was blind to how much I was eating. I mostly binged on healthy foods, apart from a couple trips to Safeway, so I couldn't understand why I was gaining so much weight. I thought I was being "good," and therefore should be losing weight.

I felt like I was dying inside. I ignored, and stopped caring about my weight, because it was too painful to acknowledge that I was becoming fat again. My perception of myself was distorted. When I was anorexic I felt fat no matter how skinny I became, and now I was blind to my weight gain. I wore baggy clothes, stopped weighing myself, and pulled my stomach in every time I looked in the mirror. I was in denial like many of us who struggle with compulsion.

When my friend Komala invited me to Mill Valley, I eagerly accepted the opportunity to live away from commune life and figure things out for myself. She got me a job as a massage therapist at a lovely spa downtown, before I even arrived! I desperately needed the change. Nonetheless, I was extremely unhappy for the first two years. I missed my lifelong, nourishing connections. I isolated myself for months at a time, and felt lonelier than ever. I didn't enjoy giving massage, I worked too hard, and at first I barely made money. I was used to being in a spiritual community, where everyone treated you like family.

Mill Valley is an affluent, athletic suburb of San Francisco, and almost everyone's skinny. Many have personal trainers, private chefs, and run, cycle, or do yoga for hours each day. I was the fattest I had ever been, close to one hundred and forty pounds, which was a lot for my small frame at 5'2, especially since it mostly settled on my hips.

My dad continued to teach me meditation, but I sobbed for hours in our weekly sessions. I'd complain about my work, and I was convinced I'd never meet the right man. I felt needy and unlovable, which can repel men across oceans, from anywhere in the world.

In the meantime, and despite all this, I built a successful massage practice. I was making decent money and could pick and choose my clients. I managed to adjust and make new friends, but in my heart I knew I was destined for more.

After a couple of years, I was making love again, and my food issues abated. I was in another passionate, committed relationship, although I knew I would never marry Alexander. He nourished and satisfied me, so I lost the weight I had gained in Sedona without even trying. We loved each other deeply and had intense sexual chemistry, but we didn't meet on other levels. Our upbringing, religion, and values were too different, and I still had too much fear of abandonment.

After a year of splitting up and getting back together in the second year of our relationship, I finally managed to end it. I've never felt so divided in my life! We had a deep emotional, passionate bond I felt I couldn't live without, and yet I knew it would never work long-term. Each time we spilt up I felt like I was dying from missing him, and each time we got back together I felt like I was lying to myself. I was tortured by a deep feeling of compromise, as I turned my back on the parts of myself that needed more than stupendous sex from a relationship.

He adored me, and did everything he could to show me his love, but I couldn't fully trust him. I knew he was faithful, but I thought it would only be a matter of time before he played around. My abandonment issues and mistrust in men ruined our relationship.

Well, it turns out I created what I feared. I was on my own again—lonely, needy, and mistrusting men. I turned to my good old friend—food. In order not to gain weight again, I joined a gym, where I developed an intense crush on my trainer. He chased me around the gym like I'd never been chased before. I became so addicted to his attention and testosterone that I worked out intensely for two and a half hours every day in order to be around him. I did everything I could to lose more weight and lower my body fat percentage, so that my definition would show. This exacerbated my obsession with food.

I was back on the rollercoaster, compulsively eating and fearing food at the same time. I reverted to starving myself during the day and bingeing at night, but strictly stuck to a low-carb, fat-free, high-protein vegetarian diet. I'd have a smoothie for breakfast and another for lunch, and then I'd binge on tofu, vegetables, fruit, and legumes, in large quantities at night. Even though it seemed like I was eating like a horse, I became skinny again. I weighed one hundred and seven pounds of muscle, with little body fat. I developed cystic acne. I believe it was because my hormones were out of balance as a result of restricting fats. Anyhow, my acne gave me another reason to feel ugly and reject myself.

My body looked better than ever, but I continued to isolate myself. I went out with a couple of guys during that time, but I couldn't even fake a smile.

Even though I was beautiful by most people's standards, I was still unhappy–lacking self-love. I was beginning to realize that my feelings of unworthiness had nothing to do with my weight. Until then, I had thought being skinny was the answer to my prayers, but now I knew my body was as beautiful as it would ever be, and I still felt unlovable.

As I realized there was no way to win, I lost control. I couldn't force myself to run, lift weights, and starve myself all day having realized that being skinny would never take away my pain.

Up until that point I had always been able to lose weight by going on a diet or exercising more, but after several months of bingeing on Bread, cheese, chips, and Chocolate, I couldn't stop eating. My insatiable monster had taken over. I was fed up with spending hours at the gym every day, feeling sick to my stomach as I tried to work off my nightly binges. Each day I promised myself never to do it again, yet each night I raided the refrigerator. I'd wake up sobbing, wanting to scream. I felt so repulsed and ashamed of myself; I wanted to crawl out of my skin. How could I continue to hurt myself with food?

I felt schizophrenic, like I was possessed at night. I wondered whether evil spirits had taken over, driving me to eat. Each morning I'd commit to a new beginning of self-care. I'd gather all my strength and reluctantly force myself to go to work. At night, it was another story. I continued to sabotage my efforts and gained weight for many months.

That was the most painful time of my life with food. Throughout my life I've switched from food to sex, and back to food, again and again. I've either been in committed relationships, making love every day, or compulsively eating mostly low-calorie foods in large quantities, over-consuming my caloric needs exponentially. Food was my savior and my enemy. When I fell in love, my man became my world.

There were several pivotal moments that gave me the courage and determination to change. I would like to say

41

one morning I woke up and saw the light. However, it didn't happen that way.

When I realized being skinny didn't make me feel any more worthy of love, my efforts to control my body were shown up as futile. I suffered the same wounds of abandonment and fear of rejection regardless. I set impossible standards for myself. No matter how skinny I became it was never good enough, so I stopped trying. There was no way to win.

I also realized that no matter how much I ate, I never felt satisfied. Food couldn't satisfy my emotional needs. I felt the same boredom, loneliness, stress, or whatever the emotional trigger was, after a packet of cookies or a Chocolate bar, as before I began eating. Nothing had changed. Occasionally the feeling of fullness temporarily averted me from my unhappiness, but never for long.

My healing actually began when my weight loss strategies of deprivation and pushing myself to extremes in exercise stopped working. But at the same time, my obsession with food climaxed! I was once again compulsively eating and steadily gaining weight. Only this time, it was worse. Without my usual strategies to control my weight, it was like the brakes had stopped working, and my foot was glued to the gas pedal– compulsively overeating, obviously flooding the engine– my body. Even though I knew that over-exercising and over- or under eating wouldn't solve the problem, I couldn't stop the behavior right away. And so, for a time, I had to suffer the consequences and feel the pain I had tried to keep at bay.

It was heartbreaking: the more effort I put into changing my eating habits, the worse they became. If it weren't for my father's belief in my potential, I would have surely given up on developing this work. How could I stand up in front of a room full of people and teach them how to transform emotional eating after I had binged the night before? He spent hours on the phone with me sobbing my way through this for years. At one point he said he didn't know how to help me any longer. He couldn't continue to listen to me cry and complain. That was the only time my father wasn't able to help. I understood. It was time to find my own answers. I was grateful he had stood by me for as long as he had. He didn't abandon me by any means; he just took a break from our weekly sessions and resumed teaching me meditation without focusing on eating.

I now recognize that even though my weight loss strategies dissolved before my overeating habits, this period was a blessing. For a while it was a scary place to be, because I hadn't yet found healthy ways to care for myself. I say a blessing because remember, my life is about awakening, going beyond my ego, following my heart versus my mind, and living through grace. If my strategies of using food to deal with my unmet needs had dissolved before my weight loss strategies, would I have sought further?

Most of us think that overeating is the problem, and under eating is victory, but that keeps us in the dichotomy! Even when I was skinny I feared the insatiable monster lurking in my subconscious ready to strike at any moment. Instead of obsessing over being too fat, I'd fixate on another imperfection. I knew it was only a matter of time before I'd start eating again. Eating like a pig and gaining weight without being able to do anything about it, at least initially, was profoundly humbling.

Though I had suffered throughout my life I had always felt superior and special. Being "the-daughter-of" two highly respected meditation teachers, and wise beyond my years, made me think that I was somehow better than others. I also always thought I would be successful, so struggling for years as I built my business, and "failed", was a rude awakening. If I had been skinny, beautiful and successful, I wouldn't have gone deeper into meditation. The sacrifice of carrying an extra ten pounds has led to staggering freedom, and a deep sense of fulfillment as I share this work. I've been immersed in meditation since birth. But even so, before I brought awareness to my eating habits, I'd get up from blissful states of peace, and go straight to the kitchen and binge.

Without truly knowing and minutely experiencing the pain of these issues I wouldn't have been able to create these meditations. I wouldn't have developed the patience and compassion necessary to help you heal. I wouldn't have practiced these meditations daily, or been continually reminded that my spiritual growth is far more important than the size of my body.

As strange as this may sound, letting myself eat without restriction led to profound acceptance. I trusted that I would find balance and learn to appreciate my body, regardless of what I weighed. I was ready to embrace my imperfections and enjoy myself, so that my next relationship could come from overflow, instead of compromise. I didn't want to fear food, or be governed by strict rules. I was determined to find balance, to make choices based on what's best for my body and connect to my inner sources of nourishment. I let myself eat all my forbidden foods, so that slowly every food became neutral. I felt the effects of various foods without judgment, so that I could give my body what it needed. I saw that every time I dieted it backfired into overeating.

I had been trapped between two excruciating, opposing forces my whole life–my insatiable appetite, and a tormenting fear of gaining weight–like a puppet on a string without any power or choice. Finally I realized that the only way I'd find peace, and fully blossom into the woman I am today, without pissing away my time and energy into food, was through meditation. Nothing else had worked. I knew it would take time to change my habits.

Transforming my relationship with food became a journey. Shifting my perspective helped me relax and in time, I began to lose weight. I stopped fighting. It was time to become centered in the middle of a craving, at the grocery store, while eating, and in social situations, so that I could consistently make healthy, empowering choices. That's what we'll be doing together throughout this process.

Chapter Two

Piggy and Watchdog: The Part That Eats With Abandon, and The Part That Controls What You Eat

I spent the next four years developing, refining and practicing these meditations. As I penetrated these issues, I identified a significant dichotomy that became a golden key. As I introduced this fundamental concept to my clients, it was received with instant recognition. Sometimes their faces lit up as if a cord of truth had been struck, giving them new insight about themselves, and their food choices.

I saw the parts of my personality that were driving my behavior with food like characters in a play— Piggy and Watchdog. I endearingly named the part that eats with abandon "Piggy" because I felt like a little Piggy every time I overate. I always wanted more. Piggy ate to fill a void, trying to make me feel better.

Whenever I swung to the other side and restricted my food choices, or went on a diet, it felt like a part of me was controlling every morsel that touched my lips. I playfully named that part Watchdog. It felt domineering, forceful, and mean for denying me pleasure. Watchdog was actually looking out for me, by watching what I ate, protecting me from gaining weight, and feeling bad about myself. Watchdog wanted me to be happy, just as much as Piggy did, in opposite ways. They both wanted me to feel good. One part tried to make me feel better by eating more, and the other by eating less.

I'm going to go into great depth of how these two parts affected my thoughts, feelings and food choices, so that you can discover whether you have some version of these parts in yourself and how they affect your food choices. Then I'll ask you to name them. I'll give you several examples to choose from, or you can come up with your own names to capture the essence of the part of you that eats with abandon, and the part that denies and controls what you eat. It's important to find names that resonate with you.

Fill in your own names as soon as they come to you. In the meantime you can use Piggy and Watchdog until we come to that section. I want to give you an opportunity to get to know them better before I ask you to name them.

I'll start with Piggy. As you read about how much I wanted to eat when I was in Piggy, and how I looked at food and life through those "eyes", see if it touches you in some way. Allow yourself to feel what I'm saying. Notice if you experience similar sensations in your body when you eat. Let the energy of the part that gets consumed with food surface, so that you can understand it more deeply. See if any of my eating habits mirror yours. Even though the manifestations of this part may be different for you, allow my discoveries to ignite your awareness, and to inspire you to discover what's true for you.

As you read, pay attention to what happens in you. Which parts resonate with you? How do you feel when you're in the part that wants to eat whatever it wants?

What do you really need when Piggy takes over? Allow its nature to be revealed to you in all its facets, so that you can become familiar with it. Identify the limited ways in how Piggy deals with your hungers, emotions, and deeper needs. You may feel compassion for yourself as you have new insights about the food choices you've been making. Even if they're not always the healthiest options, you may discover that Piggy is actually attempting to care for you. You may see things in a new light as you acknowledge the strengths and limitations of this side of you.

When I describe the restrictive, food-controller allow it to surface, so that you can get to know that side of you as well. If it's covered by the part that wants to eat, it may be a little harder for you to connect with it, but it's still there. Maybe Watchdog wants to help you find a comfortable, healthy weight, and have the energy to accomplish what's important to you in your life.

Lets go back to Piggy, so that you can experience this fully and begin to recognize that there's nothing wrong with you for overeating. There may have been good reasons behind your choices. Eating may have saved you from pain, or made it a little easier to cope with challenges when you didn't have the support you needed, or you weren't strong enough to make other choices. However, these innocent ways of coping may have become negative habits even though things may be different now. You may have more strength, emotional resilience, and resources than you realize. Life may even be going beautifully for you, and overeating may just be an old habit, hanging around you like a ghost. Perhaps you're ready to discover more fulfilling ways to satisfy your needs.

I'm here to help you find healthy, empowering ways to deal with your emotions, unmet needs, and cravings, so that you feel good— proud of your food choices. You may feel loved and cared for when you give your body what it needs.

Piggy loves the sensations of having food in my mouth. Especially when it feels like each bite is making love to my taste buds with layers upon layers of rich, full flavors. Satisfying my desires with a perfect balance of creamy, crispy, crunchy, saucy, and smooth textures, all within one bite. The only thing that matters to Piggy is how delicious the ice cream is, and how good it makes me feel. It's not concerned about how I'll feel later, or whether I was hungry to begin with. I'm completely consumed. In that moment my desire is stronger than my concern about whether my choices are healthy, or what others might think. I sweep clouds of shame under the carpet, or rapidly swallow them with another big mouthful.

When Piggy is eating, I want and need a comforting feeling of fullness in my belly. Any less than being slightly too full leaves me anxious, and craving more— feeling like I didn't get enough.

Piggy eats whenever I feel stressed, board, lonely, needy, sad, unfulfilled, or insecure. Piggy gets high from decadence, "going all the way"— deriving maximum pleasure from an abundance of endless treats. Piggy seeks immediate gratification from eating, but forgets to consider the consequences, and doesn't know when to stop. Eating is Piggy's favorite hobby. It's a social lubricant like alcohol— an easy way to connect, at least with eating buddies, who enjoy food as much as I do. My life becomes centered on food. I plan activities, and choose restaurants based on what, when, and how much I want to eat, without considering other needs.

Are there any resemblances? Are you beginning to recognize some of the ways this part influences your eating habits? What happens when you're in Piggy?

Even if you don't recognize this part in you right now, reading this may help you identify it the next time you're eating. Pay attention to your body. Notice if there's urgency, greed, or tension around food. Do you take time to chew, and savor each bite? Or do you gobble it down, without feeling satisfied? Notice whether you're hungry when you eat, or whether you eat out of boredom, because it's there, or to try and make yourself feel better. What types of foods and quantities does Piggy choose? Do you get consumed with food, or are you present, available, and connected to the people you're with while you're eating?

Some of you may identify more with Watchdog, or swing back and forth like I did. Neither one is better than the other. In fact you need both. Right now, it's important to become mindful of how these two parts affect you. Identifying them is the first step in learning how to maintain your weight naturally without dieting.

Imagine what it would be like to enjoy food without worrying about your weight, and being able to wear any size in your wardrobe, or maybe even buying smaller sizes.

When Watchdog takes over I feel starved and deprived of my favorite foods, and the joy of eating.

Watchdog convinces me that if I lose more weight I'll become lovable. Watchdog isn't interested in food.

Watchdog dominated Piggy each time I went on a diet, denying and ignoring my hunger for as long as possible. Each time I thought of eating, Watchdog would bark, warning me, as if food would destroy me. My jaw would clench up, my whole body felt tight and tense as I feared food. My breathing became shallow every time I felt Watchdog breathing down my neck, growling, cautioning me— controlling every crumb that made it onto my plate, and into my mouth. Watchdog calculated every calorie, trying to figure out which choice would make me lose more weight. I'd spend hours reading every ingredient, weighing and measuring each option before I made a decision. I would often walk away confused, and empty handed. I'd eat as little as possible, determining the degree of hunger I'd be able to tolerate for long hours until my next meal. I skipped meals as much as possible, and chewed inordinate amounts of Sugarless gum to suppress my appetite. Every time I felt hungry Watchdog distracted me by making me focus on anything other than food. For me it was obsessive exercise. I hated myself, blaming my body for wanting food.

There were always increasing numbers of bad, forbidden foods that I found gross, and even inedible. I mostly watched others eat.

Controlling myself usually worked for a while, but I wasn't happy, and it never lasted—Piggy eventually took over and binged. Watchdog pushed me beyond my comfort zone when I worked out, to the point that I resisted exercise. Watchdog made me exercise as a way to control Piggy. I didn't take time to nourish myself, and I barely saw my friends.

Under Watchdog, I didn't feel nourished by food because every time I ate, I felt restricted and ashamed for eating anything more than salad and veggies. When I went home at night and wasn't occupied by work, I'd feel needs that weren't met at work, like the need for intimacy and connection. Piggy ate to try and fill them.

When Watchdog takes over how does it affect you? Do you ever feel restricted, tense, or guilty for eating, especially when you feel like you should lose weight? Do you ever feel like you don't deserve to eat? Do you feel like a part of you is punishing you for all your indulgences? After overeating, do you swing to the other side, and watch everything you eat? Do you feel left out at social gatherings because of all your restrictions and rules about what you can, and cannot eat? Do you obsess over food, and fantasize about it, but deny yourself the pleasure of eating it? Do you worry about gaining weight, or obsess over your imperfections? Do you calculate how much you've eaten to determine whether, or when you're allowed to eat again? Do you skip meals, and ignore your hunger? Do you have an extremely limited list of foods you're allowed? Do you criticize others for what they're eating? "My God that hamburger looks disgusting! I'd never even dream of eating that!" These are all symptoms of Watchdog controlling what you eat.

After you recognize these parts in yourself its important to see whether their strategies work for you. Does dieting work? Is food fulfilling your needs? Is your behavior around food nourishing you, and giving you what you want?

It took me years to realize that blaming Piggy wasn't helpful. Most weight-loss approaches require you to get rid of Piggy and focus on Watchdog, but that doesn't give you freedom. Most people eventually swing back to the other side, getting caught in a fight between Piggy and Watchdog.

When you feel conflicted, or indecisive about what to eat, it's often because one part of you wants to make a healthy choice, and another part wants to eat whatever it wants. True?

When you commit to eating healthy and two days later you're drinking too much champagne and eating cake, Piggy's taken over. How many times have you experienced that? You've probably experienced the other side as well, when Watchdog takes charge. You finally get fed up of having ice cream and potato chips rule your life, so you go on a diet.

When you're in one side, you often forget the other side exists. When you're in Watchdog food isn't a big deal, it's easy to eat healthy. You probably can't even imagine inhaling a bag of chips, or a bar of Chocolate. Whereas when you're in Piggy you can easily become obsessed with food. You may feel like you're never going to lose weight, because you can't imagine giving up your favorite snacks.

Most of us aren't as aware when Watchdog takes charge because we don't see it as a problem. Watchdog wants us to lose weight, so that we feel better about ourselves. But when we overeat Piggy's trying to help us feel better as well. It's just that Piggy doesn't recognize the consequences of overeating because that part of us is wired for instant gratification. Its nature is to go with the flow and do what feels good in the moment. Piggy is an epicurean.

You may not swing between them the way I did. Some people spend most their lives on one side, with negligible swings related to food. If a person's in Piggy without much Watchdog, they will likely suffer life-threatening diseases associated with obesity. If a person's mostly in Watchdog, they may be malnourished, which can seriously affect their health in numerous ways. Even when one side is dominant, the other side is expressing itself in ways other than eating. For example someone might be mostly in Piggy in regards to eating, but at work they're rigid, authoritative and controlling, which are all signs of an imbalanced Watchdog.

It's usually more painful to swing back and forth than to be stuck on one side. When I'm fat, I get used to being perceived that way and dress accordingly. When I'm an extra small and get used to more male attention, and then suddenly I can't stop eating and my clothes don't fit, I go through a minor identity crisis. When I get used to eating, feeling full, and centering my life on food, and I switch back to Watchdog, it takes time to adjust to being hungry again. Suddenly I have more time, from all the hours that went into shopping, cooking, and eating.

Switching in either direction is painful and disconcerting. The benefit for me in swinging back and forth is that it illuminated the conflict between these two parts of me, and led to profound insights and freedom.

54

You may be somewhere in between, or you may lean to one side. It can also change throughout your life. Perhaps you hired Watchdog to lose weight to become more attractive to your partner, or for a special event, like a wedding, but then you reverted to Piggy when you became a parent, for example.

There's nothing inherently wrong with Piggy or Watchdog. They're both attempting to find balance. They're vital parts of us that need to be integrated, so that we can become healthy and whole.

We tend to fixate on Watchdog, because we've been conditioned by society to think that slender figures are more beautiful than voluptuous ones. Watchdog can follow a food plan perfectly by weighing and measuring food, but then Piggy suffers. That part of us needs variety and spontaneity, even though right now its impulsive nature often leads to unhealthy choices. We might see a bakery with beautifully decorated cakes, or smell freshly baked cookies, and want them, whether we've just eaten, or it's an hour before dinner! Piggy's imbalances can be irrational, impulsive, and indulgent.

It's understandable that diets make Piggy the enemy, because that part feels suffocated by rules and restrictions, so it rebels. Almost every weight loss approach focuses on enforcing Watchdog's restrictive rules and denying Piggy's desires.

We may think we haven't been successful because we haven't tried hard enough, or haven't found the right approach. "If only I could be stricter, cut out "fattening" foods, and eat smaller portions." Watchdog's strategies usually make sense and are effective for a while, but are they sustainable? What happens to Piggy? How does that part get fulfilled when you're dieting?

I know, at this point you may be thinking how can I possibility win this battle. "Is there any way I can enjoy food and maintain my weight, without one of these parts severely compromising?" Yes, this process helps you do that!

The only reason we experience both these parts negatively is because we're not connected to our deeper nature. The meditations I've created as a companion to this book bring you in touch with your heart, where you can connect with Piggy and Watchdog's essence.

I realize at this point you may be a little skeptical, wondering how any real value could come from such painful parts.

"How can there be any beauty in my insatiable monster, or my merciless food-controller? What essential purpose could they possibly be serving?"

If this is a big leap for you, read closely. You are about to be given a golden key that will transform your relationship with food, and change your life.

When we deny Piggy or Watchdog, or any part of ourselves, it expresses itself negatively. If we decide that we only like certain parts of ourselves, and reject the rest, we become divided. It would be like cutting off your left arm because it looks crooked, and keeping your right leg because you think it's beautiful, except for the knee, and trying to emphasize your best features by making them as big as possible. You'd obviously be completely handicapped and dysfunctional!

I know this sounds absurd, but this is actually what we try to do to with parts of our inner nature. We ostracize parts that aren't socially agreeable. Our minds label our own traits as good and bad, or right and wrong according to what others have taught us. "If I'm too fat I won't be loved, I won't get a job." "If I finish the food on my plate mommy will love me." "If I'm skinny I'll be the apple of daddy's eye, but other women might hate me", and on and on. The conditioning from our parents or society tells us how we should behave before we even have a chance to discover who we are.

When we have conflicting values, and one part of us suffers, we try to get rid of it, or ignore it. But in doing so, we deny some of our true values and deeper needs. Then we can never be fulfilled. It's like we're cutting ourselves into pieces. We try to only feel joyful emotions, and get rid of uncomfortable feelings, but whatever we repress eventually resurfaces in distorted ways.

We become limited when we choose to only focus on one side. Our awareness shrinks and we only experience half, or parts of ourselves. When we cling, or choose just one of these sides to approach life, we become limited. We become imbalanced, and they both express themselves negatively. It's like a bird trying to fly with one wing. We may hobble through life, but we won't thrive. Piggy has as much beauty and strength as Watchdog, in complementary ways. We need both.

We're designed to be balanced. Nature is full of opposites that create balance and harmony, like light and dark, hot and cold, expansion and contraction, and birth and death.

When we embrace Piggy and Watchdog and connect with their essence they become positive, giving us tremendous beauty and strength. Piggy's intuition is as essential as Watchdog's determination. I would have never healed, or birthed this work without both.

I hope you're beginning to recognize that there's no need to get rid of Piggy or Watchdog. They only express themselves negatively when we resist one side. As we invite them into our hearts and connect with their strengths instead of their neuroses, they purify. They become our greatest allies— working together, giving us unstoppable strength, and infinite joy.

I've listed the negative qualities of Piggy, and then Watchdog below to help you identify your imbalances. Becoming familiar with Piggy and Watchdog's imbalances in the moments they happen is the first step to transforming them and connecting with their essence.

As you read the list of qualities, notice which ones resonate with you. Take note of the qualities that ring true for you. Writing about your discoveries can be another excellent way to bring light to your issues.

Signs of An Imbalanced Piggy

- Overeating
- Craving
- Emotional
- Attached
- Distracted
- Lethargic
- Lazy
- Hopeless
- Insecure
- Needy
- Worried
- Unmotivated
- Lack of Care
- Indulgent
- Depressed
- Confused
- Indecisive
- Fearful
- Unsatisfied
- Never Enough
- Greedy
- Chaotic
- Rebellion

- Stressed
- Anti-social
- Tense
- Controlling Uptight
- Fixated
- Narrow
- Angry
- Forceful
- Analytical
- Critical
- Numb
- Judgmental
- Rigid
- Restrictive
- Limiting
- Repressive
- Tyrannical

Are you beginning to recognize imbalanced traits of Piggy and Watchdog in yourself? How do they influence your food choices? Are you mostly on one side when it comes to eating, or do you swing back and forth, between dieting and overeating like I did?

Naming The Part That Wants to Eat, and The Part That Restricts You

Now that you've had an opportunity to experience some variation of these two sides of yourself, perhaps you'd like to name them. You're welcome to continue using Piggy and Watchdog if they resonate with you.

One of my German clients named them "Miss Pinky" and "Health Monk." Another named the part that wants to eat, "Chewy" because of her incessant desire to munch on things. One client named the part that likes to eat, "Cookie Monster". In the Italian version of this book I called them Piggy and Policeman. You could call Watchdog calorie-counter if that's something you get caught in, or food-controller. You can name them after cartoon characters, animals, toys, or anything that represents the energy of these two parts.

The value of naming them is that it helps you recognize that you're much more than your desire, or aversion to food. Naming them, especially in the moment you experience their imbalances, expands your awareness, so that you can connect with your deeper nature. Naming them makes you more alert. It's like you're announcing them to yourself. Normally when they come you're not even aware of them. It helps you become mindful. To transform and become free from their negative expression, you have to recognize them first.

Read carefully, because you can't skip this next step! I made that mistake for years. This next step is what will enable you to shift from a negative state of imbalance, like feeling stressed, depressed, or apathetic to an essential state of your inner being, like joy, peace, or playfulness.

After naming the part you're caught in, or the emotion or imbalance you're experiencing, in the moment, you need to open your heart to what you're experiencing. When we become aware of something we often resist it. Saying no to any part of us is painful. When we try to get rid of what we're feeling, we're basically closing our heart to Piggy and Watchdog rejecting ourselves.

If there's only one thing you take away from this entire process, the key that will transform you more than anything is to allow yourself to be exactly as you are, each moment. Allowing yourself to be as you are, no matter what you're experiencing, happens when you open your heart to yourself. When you open your heart to Piggy and Watchdog there's immediate relief. You begin to relax. Yes, you may still feel the pain of Piggy and Watchdog, but when you're not resisting them its much less painful. The resistance to them causes even more pain. You get tense and contracted inside. Criticizing these parts creates tension. Something hardens inside when you control what you feel. You try to push them away, but you can't because they're part of you. It's frustrating.

When you embrace them, invite them into your heart, and feel them unconditionally, they soften and lose their

62

power over you. The tension, resistance, and emotional discomfort dissolve, so that your energy flows freely again. The heart is soothing and healing. Energy and emotions transform in love. It feels very different when someone is loving you, than when they criticize and reject you, doesn't it? You become defensive, or closed. The same thing happens when you reject yourself. The rejection becomes more painful than Piggy and Watchdog. Even if the pain doesn't go away immediately you'll feel better in a loving atmosphere of acceptance.

When you relax and soften you become more aware. You may feel compassion for yourself, a loving care. Your sensitivity expands, so you become more aware of the deeper nature of Piggy and Watchdog. When you're contracted you cut off from your intelligence and sensitivity. When Piggy or Watchdog take over, you need all of your inner resources.

The Essence of Piggy and Watchdog

In your heart you naturally connect to their essence, all your inner strengths become available to you. You discover what would really satisfy you, and can easily make choices that give you what you really want.

Tarika's Meditations on the Fridge guided meditations bring you deep into your heart, so that you can experience this powerful transformation. I recommend getting them, so that you can enjoy the luxury of being guided through this process.

I experienced a remarkable and unexpected reward as I relaxed with Piggy and Watchdog. I began to understand their needs and wants. I recognized the motivation behind their choices. I also saw that in spite of their admirable intentions and best efforts, they weren't giving me what I needed.

As I embraced them their true essence was revealed. I discovered their unique beauty and power. At the core, when the part that wants to eat becomes integrated, Piggy knows no boundaries, which can be incredibly positive in certain aspects of life, like lovemaking, when you need to surrender and let go of limitations to experience blissful states of pleasure. Piggy can be extraordinarily intuitive, perceptive, sensitive, and deeply in tune with others. Piggy is caring, loving, supportive, and nurturing like a parent. Piggy is flexible, yielding, cooperative, and goes with the flow, so that there's harmony. Piggy is emotionally resilient, forgiving, compassionate, understanding, and patient. Piggy listens attentively, and is genuinely interested in how others feel, so that you can easily accommodate and respond to your loved ones.

Piggy can deeply feel what you need in each moment, and can connect with infinite sources of fulfillment. Piggy's nature is carefree—more interested in the moment, rather than planning or worrying about the future. Piggy likes to "party" and enjoy life to the fullest with all its delicacies and pleasures.

Through connecting with Piggy's essence I was in touch with Watchdog's essence as well. When you connect with their essence, the strengths of the other instantly become available to you.

Watchdog's essence of clarity and single-pointedness can help you overcome numerous challenges and accomplish what seems impossible. Watchdog gives you the drive and determination to follow-through on your commitments and goals. You go for what you want and pursue your dreams, without giving up until you succeed. Watchdog is courageous, adventurous, goes into the unknown— the energy of a true pioneer and leader. Watchdog gives you individuality and the ability to take care of your own needs. You have the confidence to be yourself, without worrying about what others think.

Watchdog considers the consequences of your choices and evaluates your options to determine what's best. Watchdog isn't swayed by cravings, or influenced by others. Watchdog drinks a glass of water to ease hunger between meals, and works out whether you're in the mood, or not.

In their essence, there's harmony instead of conflict. Instead of bouncing back and forth between Piggy and Watchdog they're both present, available, working for you as partners, whenever you need them.

You don't need to waste time battling your desire for cheesecake, while grudgingly ordering fruit salad. You can make choices intuitively, based on what you need each moment. Sometimes it may be cheesecake and sometimes fruit salad. You're at peace, and more often than not, you feel like you made the "right" choice. Instead of feeling like eating healthy is a negotiation, where one part of you wins and the other part loses each time you make a food choice, you rise vertically into a transcendent state of winning, where Piggy and Watchdog are on the same team!

Their essence includes all of your strengths. Sometimes you might choose what's best for your body, and sometimes you might want to go with the flow and enjoy what everyone else is eating. It becomes a graceful dance of such synergy, that at a certain point you can't tell who's leading, or where one part begins and the other ends– like lovers merging in deep communion.

Now let's focus on their essential qualities, so that your journey becomes full of light and grace.

We're going to begin with Piggy. As you read each meditation instruction, pause for a moment and close your eyes so you can experience this. Before we begin, choose one of Piggy's innate qualities from the list below, or come up with your own to help you on your journey of balanced eating.

Piggy's Essential Qualities

- Openness
- Intuition
- Care
- Sensitivity
- Grounded
- Variety
- Pleasure
- Playfulness
- Spontaneity
- Depth
- Feeling nature
- Sensuality
- Receptivity
- Relaxation
- Carefree
- Fullness
- Responsive
- Flexible
- Nurturing
- Yielding
- Supportive
- Resting

Piggy's Essence Meditation

❖ Close your eyes and take a deep breath, breathing as fully as possible. Gently place your hand on your heart, feeling the touch of your hand taking you deeper inside, awakening your natural sensitivity.

❖ Allow yourself to sink deeper with each breath you take, melting into this inner pool of richness.

❖ Think of the quality you chose--- this quality is already within you. Connect with it. It's part of you. Notice what this quality feels like. Feel the energy of this strength expanding, filling your whole body. Perhaps you see a color or a symbol that represents this quality.

❖ Receiving this experience inside your heart, feeling nurtured and fed by your inner sources of nourishment.

Now stand up and shake your body out, so that you can connect with an essential quality of Watchdog.

Watchdog's Essence Meditation

Look at the list of Watchdog's essential qualities below and choose one you resonate with.

Watchdog's Essential Qualities

- Single-pointed
- Determination
- Clarity
- Focus
- Follow-through
- Decisive
- Strength
- Discipline
- Power Leadership
- Courage Creative
- Integrity

Take a deep breath and place your hands on your heart. Let the sounds around you, and the feeling of your own breathing take you deeper inside. Perhaps you're already noticing a shift in your energy as you prepare yourself to connect with Watchdog.

Think of the quality you chose, and say it softly to yourself. Let it ripple through your whole body. Perhaps you hear a sound, or a feeling of strength as you connect with the quality you chose. You may see a symbol or colors that embody this quality.

Feel the quality radiating through your whole body, letting it expand as it becomes stronger, and more available to you.

You can practice connecting with different qualities throughout your day, or when you need to make a food choice. The more you connect with these essential qualities the stronger your inner resources become.

Transforming Piggy and Watchdog In The Moment

Here's a story to illustrate how you can connect with an essential quality when you're out of balance. You don't need to determine which quality you need. The beauty about the heart is that it reveals what you need in each moment. Sometimes you may need to connect with an essential quality of Piggy, and at other times Watchdog . When you're in touch with any of your innate qualities, all of them become available to you. Your inner being isn't divided or conflicted by different needs. At your center there's wholeness and harmony, which includes every aspect of you, and the ability to recognize and magnetize opportunities that satisfy all your needs.

The first time I recognized Piggy's nature, was while I was running on the treadmill at my parents' house one morning before we started work on these meditations.

The garage door was open and I was facing the driveway with a gorgeous view of Thunder Mountain. I saw Prasad taking his usual morning walk at a comfortable, yet purposeful pace. I could tell he was in a state of love, caring for his body.

Watchdog was pushing me to run faster. I had forced myself to do interval training the day before, and my legs were tired. I felt irritated. I didn't even feel like running.

70

I took a deep breath and felt my heart. I gave space to the irritation, Watchdog's drive, and Piggy's discomfort.

I connected with Piggy's sensitivity, so that I could feel what my body needed. I slowed down. I let my body guide my workout. As I became present to my body, my awareness expanded and I became mindful of my surroundings. I noticed the trees, birds, and soft rays of sunlight. I changed the music to something juicy and soulful, and swung my hips from side to side, feeling sexy and alive. I was connecting to Piggy's essence.

When I got back to Mill Valley, it was more challenging to be in a state of love. Sure, some days I'd remember my experience on the treadmill and let my body guide my workout. I connected with Piggy's essence, instead of being driven by Watchdog's imbalanced expression. As I connected with Piggy's essence I connected with Watchdog's essence as well, which helped me go beyond my comfort zone just enough to improve without using force. I went for walks or ran outside, instead of fixating on my routines at the gym. I took aerobics classes, or worked out with a friend. Even though I sometimes got less of a workout, I had more fun. Soon I looked forward to my invigorating workouts again. When my body needed to rest I took a day off, so working out wasn't a drag anymore.

I'm illuminating these parts of our personality that govern our relationship with food, so that you can see them more clearly, and recognize that their negative expression is just on the surface. Deeper inside they have beautiful qualities that are essential for your life.

It seems like Piggy and Watchdog's imbalances is who they are. It's painful to have conflicting needs, and

71

to feel disconnected from the inner resources that can truly satisfy you. They take over your thoughts, actions, feelings, and hunger, but you're much vaster than their impulses. Perhaps you're starting to recognize that you're much more than that deeper inside.

I'm going to briefly share my experience of what happened when I skipped the vital step of embracing Piggy and Watchdog in their negative expression. If you already have awareness of your imbalances, but still find yourself falling into old habits, it could be because you're missing this crucial step.

Recognizing these parts in myself was a major step. As I became mindful of them I saw the dramatic, and the subtler, sneakier ways they took charge. My cravings, feelings and thoughts became clues. I'd catch Piggy salivating, or Watchdog completely detached. And yet, for a while I still fell victim to their ineffective strategies.

I was still making mindless choices because I hadn't really embraced and integrated Piggy and Watchdog. I was rejecting both these parts in myself. Instead of neutrally observing them with an open heart, which is the first step to connecting with their intrinsic power, I was subtly trying to change, or get rid of them. But the more I rejected the wounded part that sought salvation in food, by strengthening Watchdog—trying to ignore my hunger, the more needy and desperate I became. Eating was Piggy's plea for attention. Unfortunately, neglecting Piggy was the reason I went to such extremes.

It became obvious that trying to get rid of Piggy, or Watchdog wasn't working. It was a profound and pivotal turning point. I began to accept myself wholeheartedly. Even though at the time I didn't realize embracing these "animals" was the key to my freedom, there wasn't much else I could do. I stopped fighting. I stopped resisting, and allowed myself to feel whatever I was feeling, even though it was often painful. Of course I still wanted to run away, numb myself with food, or distract myself by eating and ignore what I was feeling, at times. I allowed that too.

As I made friends with Piggy and Watchdog, even though I was heavier than where I wanted to be, and I couldn't stop eating, I started to connect with their true nature. The miracle is that by relaxing with being plump, I started to lose weight!

To help you become even more familiar with these parts in yourself, I'm going to guide you through a series of meditative practices to transform your unhealthy habits into nourishing ways of caring for yourself.

As we explore each food situation, you can become aware of who is eating, or not eating. You can recognize whether you're more of a Watchdog or a Piggy shopper, which one of them cooks, orders at restaurants, and their conflicting desires in moments of cravings. There are major differences in how, and what we eat depending on whether we're in Piggy or Watchdog. When I'm in Watchdog I can eat 3-5 nuts, whereas when I'm in Piggy I can easily eat a whole bag!

As you come in touch with their essence, you'll instinctively make choices from understanding and care, rather than greed and self-denial.

Some of the practical activities require you to connect with the essential qualities of Watchdog, and others focus on Piggy. I've defined each one to make it easy for you. In the beginning it can be helpful to focus on one at a time, but ultimately you'll need to connect with both. But don't worry because when you're in touch with their essence the other is right there. You can trust, this process will work for you too.

You may notice that there are more Mindful Watchdog Activities than Mindful Piggy Playtimes because many of us, particularly those of us who overeat, spend more time in Piggy, and need practice connecting with Watchdog's essence. As you become aware of how they can either control you negatively, or transform you positively, you'll be motivated to practice these meditations. As you connect with their true power and intrinsic beauty you may even forget you had a problem!

Chapter Three

Meditation Frees You From Dieting

Now that you have a sense of how Piggy and Watchdog's essential qualities bring you into balance, I'm going to guide you through a series of simple, yet highly effective heart meditations. Remember to shift from Piggy and Watchdog's negative expression to their essence; you need to start with the heart. Then I will guide you into several of Piggy and Watchdog's most vital qualities for making healthy food choices.

These meditations connect you with your innate body wisdom so that you can discover what works for your body, and choose nourishment that satisfies you. There isn't one way of eating that works for everyone, as we're all unique. We have different needs, preferences, habits, schedules, challenges, and resources. And your needs are always changing, so to make the right choices consistently, it's important to tune in to your body and intuitive wisdom.

I'm not going to ask you to starve yourself, or give you a restrictive weight-loss plan. You'll likely lose weight as you make healthier choices, but for now I suggest you forget about weight loss. Focus on foods and activities that make you feel good, rather than obsessing over your weight. These meditations connect you with your body wisdom, so that you can maintain your weight without dieting.

What is Meditation?

There are many ideas about meditation. Meditation is usually associated with finding inner peace, or quieting your mind and becoming free of thoughts. The ultimate goal of meditation has been to discover who you really are, often referred to as enlightenment.

Throughout the ages, religions and spiritual teachers around the world have created countless meditation techniques to produce these results. Sitting silently and watching your breath is among the most universal techniques. However, many people feel frustrated when they become too focused on quieting their minds. These techniques give you the benefits of meditation without having to control your thoughts.

When you first turn your attention inward you may be distracted, or your attention may wander. You may find yourself thinking about a particular event or fantasizing about food. Don't worry; this happens to all of us at times, especially in the beginning. When you notice your attention wander, simply bring yourself back to the meditation without judging. Your ability to be present will naturally grow over time.

The idea that your mind should be silent is probably one of the primary reasons most people give up on meditation, or don't even try it. It's natural to be distracted by thoughts. The good news is it's not a problem. These meditations expand your awareness so that it's vast enough to include your thoughts, cravings, and deeper nature.

Deeper nature is another way of saying soul or inner being. I'll be using the words interchangeably. I prefer deeper nature or inner being, because those terms aren't as loaded with preconceived ideas, but please use whatever words are meaningful to you. I'm referring to that which is beyond your thoughts, emotions, and mindsets.

You don't need to attain an ultimate state of enlightenment to successfully change your habits. You'll likely experience many benefits from these meditations, like blissful states of silence, love, and profound connections to yourself and others, as a bonus. These meditations aren't designed to teach you how to control your thoughts. They're designed to transform your emotions around food, and connect with your wisdom, so that you can make healthier choices without struggle.

In a nutshell, meditation connects you to your inner nature, which includes Piggy and Watchdog's essential qualities. As you become aware of your eating habits, you'll notice subtle and profound changes in how you respond to everyday and challenging food situations, and to life in general.

Tarika Lovegarden's Approach

Our approach to meditation is to expand your awareness through heart meditations. Through expanding your awareness you connect with your deeper nature. Awareness illuminates deeper dimensions inside, so that you can discover who you really are.

The way awareness grows is by being aware. As you become aware of your body, feelings, and thoughts, your awareness expands. Even just a few moments of being aware each day significantly expands your awareness. As you become more aware you can easily determine what you need, without having to follow dietary rules. These meditations connect you to your innermost qualities, like courage, power, strength, and love, to name a few. Many refer to the expression of these essential qualities as our soul.

Your inner strengths are your unique way of expressing these virtues. For example one of your strengths might be cooking, and you express essential qualities of love and care when you cook. Another person might express love and care as a nurse. We all have the same qualities inside; we simply use them in different ways. Talented parents express their creativity in different ways. One might have a creative gift in carving vegetables into enticing, fun shapes, and another parent might be creative in how they help their children with homework, by putting on music, or drawing pictures to illustrate things, so that their children enjoy the process of learning. Both parents are expressing the essential quality of creativity in their strength in parenting.

These meditations connect you with your inner strengths and intrinsic virtues, so that it becomes easy to make the right choices. It's not important for you to differentiate between them. I'll be using the terms interchangeably, as they're essentially the same. The goal is simply to connect with your inner power, love, and wisdom, which have as many expressions, as there are shades of color. As you take time to connect with these inner resources, and you give power to your strengths instead of feeding old habits, it becomes easier to make the right choices. You'll be amazed as you discover what works for your body and find new ways to fulfill your needs.

As you increase your awareness, you'll notice improvements in your food choices and in how you feel about your body. Being aware of something increases your sensitivity and allows you to experience what you are aware of fully. For example, by being aware of your body you become attuned to what your body needs. As you connect to your body wisdom, there's a refinement in your food choices and how you care for yourself. It's thrilling to see yourself transform as a result of this increased sensitivity. You'll notice a difference in how you eat, bathe, exercise, and sleep, simply by becoming aware.

Heart Gives You Freedom

Awareness without heart would make you miserable! You're probably aware of your unhealthy habits, but haven't found a way to change them. You've probably tried numerous approaches, only to fall victim to your cravings again, and again, and again. I certainly have. Thankfully I became so fed up of dieting, bingeing, taking herbal laxatives, and forcing myself to run, that I pursued meditation. The key is to tune into your bodies' needs through loving care, rather than trying to control and deprive yourself.

Without these meditations I wasn't able to stick with the foods, quantities, and meal times that were good for my body, which is probably the case for many of you. You probably have more nutritional knowledge than most yet still battle unhealthy habits. Your heart brings you into a sweet spot where you can follow your wisdom and experiment with nutritional principles to discover what works.

These meditations are designed to open your heart center, also known as the heart chakra, which is located in the center of your chest. Everyone experiences their heart. When people say, "I love you from the bottom of my heart," they're not referring to their physical heart, they're referring to their heart center, perhaps without even realizing it.

The easiest way to connect with your heart is through your senses. I'm going to guide you into three short meditations, so that you can experience this. We'll begin with the feeling sense.

Feeling Your Heart Meditation

This meditation opens your heart and increases your ability to feel your body. This helps you to feel, and become attuned to your needs, so that you can make choices that are right for you. There are several ways to use these meditations. The easiest way is to simply read through them. Believe it or not, your heart will listen, and you'll likely feel its response. If you like you can briefly pause and close your eyes between each set of instructions to experience them fully. Please experiment to find what works for you.

My recorded guided meditations, also entitled "Tarika's Meditations on the Fridge" that accompany this book, practically guide you through my step-by-step process, so that you can make healthy food choices in each food situation. I recommend listening to them as much as possible. You'll transform your body each time

80

you make healthy choices, instead of getting caught in mindless eating habits.

- ❖ Adjust your body so that you feel comfortable and relaxed. Place your hands on your heart, in the center of your chest. Feeling the warmth or coolness of your hands gently touching your heart.
- ❖ Take deep breaths, feeling the rise and fall of your chest as you breathe; carrying you deeper inside.
- ❖ Feel your hand touching your heart with sensitivity and care. Feeling the flow of energy, like gentle waves, opening your heart with each breath you take.
- ❖ Continue breathing in this way, feeling your heart, for as long as you like.

How do you feel? You can feel your heart in any moment. Each time you connect with your heart your experience will deepen, giving you greater sensitivity to respond to your needs with loving care.

Listening from the Heart Meditation

This meditation opens your ability to listen deeply. Listening to the sounds around you, while feeling your heart naturally brings you into the moment. Instead of your mind filtering and interpreting what you hear, your heart is listening. When you listen from your heart you receive your inner voice, and can intuitively make the right choices.

❖ Find a comfortable position. Place your hand on your heart, and take a deep breath. Feeling your hands resting on your heart touching you deep inside.

❖ Listening to the sounds around you – feeling the vibration of the sounds in your heart, awakening a natural sensitivity in you, so that you can receive the intuitive wisdom of your heart.

❖ Ask your heart, do you have a message for me related to my body and food? Is there a particular food you need more, or less of? Do you need more rest, movement, or some other type of care or nourishment? Taking time to receive your intuitive wisdom. These messages may come to you as a vision or symbol, an inner voice, or a feeling receiving this now.

❖ Resting here for as long as you like, continuing to receive your own wisdom.

How is it to receive the wisdom of your heart? You can practice connecting with your heart any time you need inner guidance. Begin by listening to soft music or sounds in nature, as that will naturally open your heart. Then ask your heart to reveal its wisdom.

You can also ask a specific question. Remember you may receive your wisdom through an inner voice, you may get a sense for something, or you may see an image, like a green or red light indicating whether you should eat, or do something, or not. Each of you will receive your intuitive wisdom differently. Sometimes it's not so clear in the beginning, but it will get stronger and more available to you each time you connect with it. I recommend starting with simple things, like what to order at restaurants, or what to eat for breakfast to develop trust in your inner wisdom.

Seeing from the Heart Meditation

This meditation opens your inner vision, so that you can see your true nature and connect with your inner strengths. You have everything you need inside to restore your body to health.

- ❖ Take a deep breath, and close your eyes, allowing the energy from your eyes to turn inward. Place your hands on your heart; feeling the soothing, calming energy inside your heart.
- ❖ Imagine your heart is a flower---- Allowing this image to come to you naturally. Notice the shape, color, and fragrance of the flower. Imagine that you can reach inside and gently touch the flower. How does it feel?
- ❖ This flower represents a quality of your heart. The heart has many expressions of love, care, wisdom, and inner strengths. How does it feel to connect with your heart in this moment?
- ❖ Continue to feel these inner qualities as you look at the flower of your heart. You can open your inner vision whenever you need, simply by imaging your heart as a flower. You may see other metaphors or symbols representing your inner strengths.

How is it to open your inner vision and experience one of the many qualities of your heart? You can do this meditation whenever you like. The more you practice connecting with your heart, the stronger it will become. It's like building a new muscle. Pretty soon, you'll be feeling your heart spontaneously throughout your day. The secret to transformation is your heart. That's what makes this program effective. The heart makes your experience warm and enjoyable. In your heart you perceive yourself with compassion, instead of judgment.

Having an awareness of your unhealthy habits without the transformative power of your heart isn't enough to change them. When you eat too much ice cream you know you'll eventually gain weight, don't you? Are you able to stop? Perhaps at times, but what about the times you can't, even when you're miserably gaining weight? The heart has space for your desire for more, and enables you to feel how ice cream affects you, so that you can make choices from understanding and care.

We all know what we "should" be eating; yet we can't follow through. When you make changes from loving care, it feels good. Hence you're more likely to maintain those changes until they become healthy habits. Nobody likes to suffer. Your heart and inner strengths make healthy eating fulfilling and pleasurable.

Your heart enables you to feel the impulses that make you reach for ice cream and let them pass without indulging. It expands the moment, giving you space from your old habits, so that you can make new choices. The heart is timeless. Your heart gives you time to consider the consequences of eating ice cream and whether it's worth it. Normally, our habits take over before we realize we have a choice. Your heart pauses and expands the moment, so that you can decide whether, what, and how much you want to eat.

As you become more aware, you'll notice that sometimes you eat when you're not even physically hungry. Having an awareness of what makes you eat, and whether it fulfills you, gives you good reasons to change. As your awareness grows, you'll lose interest in foods and quantities that make you feel uncomfortable.

A while ago, I had such a strong craving for Chocolate that I bought some on my way home. I knew it was probably the beginning of a binge, but instead of going into the negative expression of Watchdog and trying to force myself to drive straight home, where I would have eaten other things anyway, I went with it.

When I noticed that I was frantically swallowing semi-chewed bites, without even enjoying it, I slowed down. I didn't condemn myself, as that would have likely made me rebel and eat even more. A few pieces later I stopped, half way through my favorite Chocolate bar! Normally, I would have eaten the whole thing. I stopped because of awareness. By slowing down I became present to my body and realized that it was an emotional craving, and Chocolate wasn't making me feel better. I got up, and threw the rest away, so that I wouldn't be tempted later, and went to bed.

The loving atmosphere of your heart is what enables you to break old habits. Your strengths make it easy for you to throw food away when you need to, without feeling like you're losing something.

The Essence of Your Soul

Connecting with Piggy and Watchdog's essential qualities enables you to make the right choices, and it's fulfilling! Spiritual seekers have known this for centuries: everything we're seeking is within us. Relaxation already exists in you! You don't need a bag of potato chips to relieve your stress. A brownie can't give you love and connection. The experiences you're longing for: the love, connection, and harmony, are at your center waiting for you. You have everything you need. When you're connected to your soul, you take better care of yourself because it feels good, not because you're afraid of gaining weight.

You don't have to "go" anywhere to connect with your inner strengths. They are here. They are you. We become disconnected from our nature because we're in a habit of seeking fulfillment outside ourselves. When you open your "inner eyes," like we did in the Seeing From the Heart meditation, you come in touch with your true power. All of your senses can turn inward and open, so that you can perceive yourself, others, and life with clarity.

Paying attention to what you are hearing, seeing, and feeling as you eat connects you to your body wisdom. Your heart and inner strengths give you the clarity and sensitivity to know what's right for you, so that you can make empowering choices. Right now, you'll probably find that oftentimes you don't have choice! One moment you're committed to a healthy way of eating, and the next moment you're indulging, feeling guilty and ashamed. Something just takes over.

Your heart enables you to come into the moment, so that you can have what you really want. Sometimes you may choose a brownie; but you can do so consciously. The next moment you might choose tofu and kale. If you really want a brownie, and you give yourself permission to enjoy it, you're much more likely to feel satisfied. You won't need to promise yourself to go to the gym, or binge to deal with your guilt and shame. You can enjoy the brownie and then tune into your body to determine what you need to maintain balance. From a meditator's perspective, there aren't any good or bad foods. The only thing that matters is that you have the freedom to choose what's right for you!

I'm going to guide you through another short series of meditations, so that you can experience the inner strengths that will help you on this journey, beginning with your body wisdom.

Heart Connects You to Your Body Intuition

Body intuition is another way of saying body wisdom; only I think the term more accurately describes how you receive your body's wisdom, which is intuitively. Our bodies have a natural intelligence. Our bodies know what we need to feel satisfied, and to maintain a healthy weight. Our bodies communicate with us constantly throughout the day. Sometimes we simply can't hear this wisdom or don't know how to interpret it.

Your intuition interprets these important messages, so that you can understand them. Intuition is your ability to perceive life, others, and yourself, beyond what the eyes can see. It's another quality of the heart. The mind perceives things based on knowledge and past experiences. Your intuition can perceive things before they even happen!

Have you ever known something was going to happen ahead of time, or predicted what someone was going to say? Everyone has intuition; but we don't always listen, trust, or follow it, especially when Piggy's craving.

Body Intuition Meditation

This meditation connects you to your body intuition, so that you can recognize what your body needs and make satisfying choices. Pause between each set of instructions to give yourself time to receive your intuition.

❖ Take a deep breath and close your eyes, allowing your attention to turn inward. Place your hand on your heart, feeling how your heart responds to your touch.

❖ Listen to the sounds around you, allowing them to take you deeper inside. As you connect with your heart perhaps you see soft light, or an image revealing your inner treasures.

❖ Take deep breaths into your heart. As you breathe and feel your heart, you're naturally connecting with the intuitive wisdom of your heart so that it becomes easy to recognize what your body needs. You can ask your heart to reveal what your body needs to come into balance.

❖ Receive what comes to you. You may see yourself eating a particular food, or caring for yourself in a new way. You may feel like your body needs to move, or rest. You might receive a message, or hear the voice of your intuition, communicating what you need. Or perhaps you feel warm and nourished, as you see yourself preparing a healthy meal.

❖ Continue to take deep breaths, receiving your body intuition in whatever ways they come to you.

Sometimes your body's messages will make sense to you, and sometimes it takes time to recognize what you need. I encourage you to practice connecting with your body intuition whenever you can. The meditations in the following chapters will give you opportunities to practice using your intuition to make healthy food choices in different situations.

There's no "one-diet-fits-all," so you need to connect with your body intuition in order to recognize how different foods affect you, so that you can make sustainable changes. Your inner strengths enable you to make empowering choices through your own understanding, which is far more powerful than any recommendation I, or anyone else, could give you.

Your body intuition gives you the clarity to know what's right for you, even when your needs change. Sometimes you may need to go for a walk, and other times you may need to rest, or go out to dinner with a friend. Diet books that require you to make a list of things you'll do each time you have a craving usually aren't effective long term. It's helpful to brainstorm and have a healthy eating plan, but you still need to tune into your body and deeper needs each time you have a craving to determine what you need.

Heart Connects You to Determination

This is another strength that will help you create healthier habits and carry you through the challenges of balanced eating and weight loss. It's an essential quality of Watchdog, very different from willpower and control. Sometimes it takes determination to allow Piggy 'surges, while choosing foods that give you what you really want, instead of trying to fulfill Piggy's food fantasies.

There are many moments in transforming your food issues that requires this power that you have inside. Determination enables you to wait for meals or treats, so that you're not taken over by your desire for instant gratification. I still need to connect with discipline to wait to eat until my body's hungry, or to pass by temptations that make me gain weight, and leave me unsatisfied.

Determination Meditation

- ❖ Take a moment to connect with your heart by taking a deep breath. If you like, you can place your hand on your heart to help you settle in. Your touch can easily evoke the familiar energy of warmth, wisdom and the inner beauty of your heart.
- ❖ Think of an area of your life in which you're determined, or think of someone close to you who's determined. What do you experience when you see yourself, or someone else expressing this quality? Is there a feeling in your body? Do you see an image that represents this quality? Softly whispering determination to yourself can evoke this energy in you.
- ❖ You can trust your heart to reveal your determination in a way that's natural for you. Connecting with this energy inside you now.
- ❖ Take a deep breath and let it vibrate through your whole body. Now imagine yourself making a food choice as you connect with your determination to have what's important to you.

Connect with determination whenever you need a boost of strength. I love to connect with it while walking. You may like to swing your arms and increase your pace, so that determination can energize your whole body. A two-minute determination walk from your car to the grocery store can help you make healthier choices.

Find easy ways to connect with determination, so that it becomes more accessible when you need to make healthy food choices.

Heart Connects You to Loving Care

Love and care are qualities of the heart. You already connect with these qualities in many moments during your day without even realizing it. When you bring attention to those moments, your inner qualities expand and become more available to you. Loving care transforms how you eat, care for yourself, and how you feel about your body. Words can't even describe the healing power of your heart!

Loving Care Meditation

- ❖ Take a deep breath into your heart, allowing the feeling of your breathing to bring you inside. Feeling how each breath creates more space inside, gently expanding your heart. As you feel your heart you may already have feelings of tenderness, love and care.
- ❖ Take a moment to remember a time when you lovingly cared for yourself, someone close to you, or a pet. Feel what it's like to care in this way. Perhaps you feel an expansion inside, or a warm, soothing energy radiating from within, or you see yourself attentively caring for someone.
- ❖ Take a deep breath and let this feeling fill your whole body. See yourself selecting foods, and eating while connecting with the loving care within you.

My favorite times to connect with loving care is in the shower, brushing my teeth, moisturizing my body, and while cooking. When do you naturally feel this quality inside? Find little moments throughout your day to connect with loving care, so that it becomes more and more available to you.

The Power of the Moment

The heart exists in the moment. Whenever you're connecting to your heart, you're in the moment. You can feel your heart in this moment, simply by resting a hand on your heart as you continue reading.

The moment is the "time" to make empowering choices, especially when you're about to get taken over by old habits. When you feel an urge to eat you usually bounce back and forth between the past and the future. When you get taken over by habits from the past and eat for emotional nourishment, it can feel like you're never going to change. When you bounce into the future, you might plan and strategize, promising yourself you'll go on a diet tomorrow as a way to avoid feeling fat.

Perhaps you look into the future and see a dark road that doesn't go anywhere, because of all your failed attempts at losing weight. Or you look at your future optimistically and fantasize about being skinny, but your resolutions never materialize because you can't follow through. Habits are born from the past. They're an accumulation of unconscious impulses, a crystallization of past experiences that prevent us from being in the moment.

How many times have you found yourself in the exact same place, standing at the kitchen counter, or watching TV, eating? Or perhaps your habits take over at a certain time of day, and you eat Chocolate every afternoon or ice cream into the wee hours of the night. When we repeat the past and eat unconsciously, it can often feel like something just takes over, like someone else is eating. The more we do something, the stronger a habit becomes. Eating Chocolate one time is very different from eating Chocolate every afternoon for months on end.

I've given you a few examples, with which you may or may not relate. The point is for you to recognize that when you go on automatic you're in the past or the future, rationalizing or strategizing. Your habits, cravings, diet strategies, and weight fluctuations repeat themselves again, and again. The food or time of day might change. I've switched from cheese to Chocolate and from mid-afternoon to evening, but the compulsive energy is the same, until you connect with your heart and deeper nature.

Dieting is like rearranging furniture. You might successfully break a habit temporarily, but if you haven't gotten rid of the uncomfortable couch, your old habits will likely take over again, reupholstered. Your inner strengths and soul only exist here-now. They don't exist in the past or the future. Success is in the here-now, hence the title of Eckhart Tolle's renowned book, The Power of Now.

The past and future only have the power you give them, meaning you have the freedom to give into your cravings, or to make a choice that feels good. You're only in touch with your "real" power when you're in the moment. Being in the moment is meditation.

Chapter Four

Satisfying Your Body Nutritionally

If you already have a healthy foundation, and need support in specific areas like cravings, the guided meditations and practical activities may be sufficient. If that's the case, you can skip this one, and continue with the next chapter. If you've struggled, like I have, I recommend experimenting with these nutritional principles to see how they benefit you.

Since Piggy and Watchdog are our greatest influencers when we select food, I'll give you the simplest and most beneficial suggestions, without going into too much nutritional science. Even though most people are familiar with basic principles like drinking water and eating whole foods, I've found that many don't follow them consistently.

As you read this chapter choose one or two principles to focus on at a time, or come up with your own, to help you establish a new way of living. It's better to make doable, sustainable changes than to follow restrictive diets, and revert to old habits. To make things easy I recommend focusing on changing one habit at a time. That way you won't overwhelm yourself, and your success in making simple changes will give you the strength to let go of the stronger attachments you have to certain foods.

When your body's nutritionally satisfied, it's much easier to make healthy choices. For overeaters, the emotional, psychological and behavioral impulses are challenging enough to overcome without physical cravings. Nutrition brings your body into balance, so that you don't crave unhealthy, or large quantities of food, at least not physically.

Nutritionists agree on the benefits of eating whole foods. If the only change you made were switching from refined foods to eating primarily whole, minimally processed foods, in reasonable quantities, you'd have excellent results.

Whole, Unprocessed Foods

Whole foods are intact, as close as possible to their form found in nature. Processed foods have been altered in some way: refined, ground, juiced, dried, roasted, etc. Minimally processed foods retain most of their nutritional value, as their fiber and nutrients are generally intact. Some nutrients get lost through exposure to light and heat during processing, so they're not as nutritious as whole, unprocessed foods, but they're superior to refined foods. Refined foods have been processed and reduced from their original form, and stripped of vital nutrients. Manufacturers often add back synthetic nutrients to make up for the lost nutrients, but synthetic nutrients are less available for our bodies to absorb, and, in fact, potentially toxic. Refining and processing foods destroys phytonutrients, taking away the synergistic effect of whole foods.

Fiber is removed from most refined grain products. Refined foods are more clogging and constipating, spike our blood Sugar, trigger cravings, make us retain water, and cause weight gain. Without fiber and vital nutrients, foods aren't as satiating, so we generally consume more calories. In other words, fiber helps us feel full, and vital nutrients send our bodies the signal that we are getting what we need, and so our hunger naturally abates.

There's no right way of eating that works for everyone. The only thing I recommend to everyone is to eat whole, unprocessed, or at least minimally processed foods as much as possible. As for the rest, I think it largely depends on your biochemical individuality, which you can discover for yourself quite naturally, as you pay attention to how you feel when you eat various foods.

I'll be helping you connect with your body wisdom, so that you can discover which foods are right for you. You'll be amazed as your body tells you what it needs, and elated by the results of following its wisdom.

Whole foods are more nutritious, satisfying, easier to digest, metabolize and eliminate, and not as addictive! Most refined foods are designed to make you crave more, starting with their lack of fiber and micronutrients. Advertisements that say, "You won't be able to stop after one bite" are true! Food companies have teams of scientists observing the effects of substances on appetite, and the feel-good chemicals in our brain that make foods addictive. They're paid to figure out which ingredients to use, so that you literally can't stop eating their products!

When you eat a bag of chips or a pack of cookies, it's not because there's something wrong with you, or that you lack willpower. Those foods are chemically addictive, and some of us are more susceptible to food addiction than others. It's very possible that this susceptibility may be linked to the nature of the issues that cause us to seek comfort from food in the first place. I think genetics and physical imbalances play a role in what substances we become addicted to, but our conditioning and values influence us as well. Most people do best when they limit their consumption of refined Sugars and grain products.

Our bodies haven't adapted to refined, man-made foods, or to the large quantities we consume. In our hunter-gatherer days, we ran miles for an animal to be shared amongst many, and climbed tall trees to pick fruit, which took much more energy than walking from a parking lot to the grocery store and pushing a cart around. Our bodies became efficient at storing calories in order to survive periods of famine or reduced availability of foods. No one had a fridge or freezer to store food back then!

These survival mechanisms that kept our species alive for centuries haven't gone away in response to our modern overconsumption of food. Our genetic virtues of storing calories are encumbering; at least for those of us who overeat.

One of the values of eating whole foods is that they're satiating. Your weight is influenced by your caloric intake in relation to your caloric need. Undereating usually isn't a sustainable solution, so you need to find ways to feel satisfied with less food if you want to lose, and maintain your weight. Eating whole foods is an excellent first step, because it helps you transition from addictive, fattening foods.

After you have found whole food replacements for your refined favorites, you can consider the ratio of your caloric intake and expenditure. I resisted counting calories, but I recently experimented with recording everything I ate. There are numerous free nutrition software programs online that calculate your caloric intake and needs, along with your macronutrient percentages, which I'll explain shortly.

If you want to be able to eat whatever you want and maintain or lose weight, measuring and recording what you eat can be a good option. If you really want ice cream, you might choose to eat less for dinner, or have a smaller quantity so that you don't exceed your caloric needs. Or you may look at the caloric content and lose interest because it isn't worth the fleeting pleasure. I sometimes entered a food before I ate it to see how it would affect the balance. Recording what you eat gives you tremendous awareness about quantities, and the ability to determine which foods are the most satiating for the least amount of calories, quickly.

If you've struggled with yoyo dieting and weight fluctuations, it's best to start by determining what, and how much you can eat to stabilize your weight. Once you discover what your body needs to maintain its weight, you can consider eating less if you still feel like you want to lose weight. Then you're more likely to maintain your weight loss, because you'll have the experience of eating what your body needs to maintain homeostasis. Once you achieve your goal weight, you can play with the balance of, how many "festive" foods you can enjoy, how often, and in which quantities, without gaining weight. It's healthier and better for your self-esteem to be stable, even if you're heavier than where you want to be, than to fluctuate. It's heartbreaking to gain weight, especially if you've put a lot of effort into losing weight, isn't it? Once you relax with food and can confidently choose what to eat, you can decrease your intake.

If you just want to lose weight and haven't swung to extremes, you may be ready to start eating less right away. Please do what feels right.

Mindful Watchdog Activity: Enjoy Whole, Unprocessed Foods and, or Track Your Food

There isn't one system that works for everyone. Some people have extraordinary results from using online software that calculates the caloric content of the foods you consume, and your expenditure based on your activity level, age, sex, and size. Others become more obsessed with food when they track it. If that's true for you than you'll likely have better success with the whole foods approach. You still need to be mindful of quantities. You can easily gain weight from eating too many nuts, fruit, and whole grains. However, most people feel much more satisfied with whole foods, than refined foods. Refined Sugars and grains pack on weight exponentially faster than whole foods.

Mindful Watchdog Activity: Track Your Food (if it helps you)

Write down, or photograph, everything you eat for at least twenty-four hours. By tracking what you eat and how you feel afterwards, you can discover the foods and quantities that work best for you. The longer you do this the better. Some people adopt tracking their food as a lifestyle. You can even do it on your phone, with apps like My Fitness Pal, Fitbit, and Sparks People to name a few. This is most effective when you are ruthlessly honest in writing down everything you eat. Yes, that includes the bits of toast left on your kid's plate when you clean up, and the bite of your coworker's doughnut. You might be surprised by how much food you're not accounting for when you take time to record it.

Mindful Watchdog Activity: Enjoy Whole, Unprocessed Foods (even if you track your caloric consumption I recommend this for everyone!)
Look at the refined foods you ate and think of an alternative whole food to replace it with. For example, if you ate a pastry for breakfast, try making Oatmeal from old-fashioned, steel-cut, or, better yet, rolled Oats. Can you see how each suggestion gets closer to the whole, unprocessed form? You may not think there's much difference, but refined foods can make us lethargic and depressed, diminishing our zest for life!

I used to say things like, "It's the same ingredients, so I might as well eat whatever I want. A granola bar is made from oats, how's that different from oatmeal?" Even though it may be the same amount of calories, they're very different! I recognized the difference when I paid attention to how I felt after eating oatmeal instead of a granola bar. I felt more satisfied and didn't even think about food until later in the afternoon. Whenever I ate a granola bar, I'd usually want another, or something else, before I even finished the first one.

Then enjoy as many of your new, whole-food alternatives as possible, and notice how you feel. Take notes in a journal, if you have one. You can combine the approaches and track your food online if that's helpful.

The Ideal Balance of Macronutrients for Your Body

Macronutrients are the three major components of food that give us energy. Even though most foods contain all three, to varying degrees, foods are categorized based on their highest macronutrient content. They're either considered a protein, fat, or carbohydrate.

For example, meat, fish, eggs, dairy, legumes (also high in carbohydrate), and nuts (also high in fat) are considered proteins. Proteins are our building blocks, needed to make enzymes, antibodies, and hormones, and build and repair muscles, nerves, and cells. Proteins are made up of twenty-two amino acids, eight of which are essential, meaning our bodies can't produce them. We need to get them from food.

Protein is a magical food for sustainable weight loss, especially in combination with the right amount, and types of carbohydrates and fats. When I eat protein I feel fuller with fewer calories than with any other macronutrient.

Common sources of protein:

Meat, poultry, fish, dairy (cheese, yogurt, kefir, cottage cheese, etc.), eggs, legumes, protein powders, and micro-proteins (bee pollen, fresh or powdered green grass juices, and Brewers' yeast).

Don't go protein crazy though. You can gain weight by eating too much of any macronutrient. Balance and caloric consumption are paramount.

For months I ate a fat-free lunch of protein and salad but would get hungry two to three hours later, and couldn't make it until dinner without snacking, and often bingeing. I realized protein and plain salad wasn't enough to carry me through the day. After adding cooked vegetables and moderate amounts of healthy fats, I felt satisfied. I enjoyed nourishing dinners without snacking, and lost weight by eating more at lunch, instead of less.

Cutting out any macronutrient usually leads to imbalances and cravings. The timing, size, and balance of your meals can be significant. When I ate fruit for breakfast, and a light lunch, with only tea and water in between, I binged at night. When I added protein and fat to my breakfast and increased my lunch, I felt satisfied with a reasonable dinner and stopped bingeing. Eating bigger, balanced meals throughout the day enabled me to eat less overall.

High-protein diets can be a fast way to lose weight, but they're usually not sustainable. Whenever you cut out, or severely limit any food group, you become deficient in certain nutrients. High-protein diets tend to lack fiber, vitamins and minerals found in grains, beans, fruit, and vegetables, because of their restriction on carbohydrates.

Carbohydrates are our main source of energy, especially for our brain and nervous system. Carbohydrates are classified as simple Sugars and complex starches, depending on their molecular structure and how they're metabolized. Plants produce carbohydrates, so most carbohydrates are plant foods. Fiber is a complex carbohydrate, so in their whole, natural form, carbohydrates contain fiber, which is necessary for satiety and elimination.

High-carbohydrate diets tend to lack protein, which often causes cravings, depending on your biochemical individuality. When I don't eat enough protein I can easily eat a thousand calories and still feel hungry. Others do well on high-carbohydrate diets. Pay attention to how you feel when you eat protein, carbohydrates, lots of fat, a little fat, or fat-free meals, so that you can find the most energizing and satiating foods for your body.

Carbohydrates affect our mood, and subsequent food choices, more than any other macronutrient. When I overeat carbs I get depressed, and it takes much longer to get back to healthy eating. Refined carbohydrates can be evil, due to the rollercoaster combination of how they affect blood Sugar and their lack of micronutrients. In nutrition we refer to refined carbohydrates as "empty calories" or "negative nutrition," because they take more micronutrients to digest and eliminate than they provide. As such, I find it's most important of all to make good choices around carbohydrates, perhaps also because they are so easily available.

My preferred sources of Carbohydrates:

Dark leafy greens, vegetables, salads, seaweeds, fruit, whole grain, and legumes (which are high in fiber and protein. They can be considered a protein or a carbohydrate because they contain a fair amount of both).

Fat-free diets can also be a fast way to lose weight, but like high-protein diets, they usually aren't sustainable and often cause powerful cravings. I spent a couple of years on a fat-free diet when I moved back to Sedona. After a fast, initial weight loss I had the strongest cravings in my life. I gained fifty-five pounds because I literally couldn't stop eating. My body was starving for nutrition. I was already very skinny to begin with, as it was after my anorexic phase, but I'm sure the lack of dietary fat was one of the culprits.

As a child I made poor food choices because I felt abandoned and stressed emotionally. But my compulsive eating habits didn't begin then, even though I ate lots of sweets. They started after under-eating and following a fat-free diet. Our brains use more fat than any other part of our body. They run on glucose, but they need fat for many important functions.

Fats are satiating, and help the nerves in our stomach send the signal of fullness to our brain. Fats are the most concentrated source of calories (nine calories per gram, versus four for protein and carbohydrates), so they are easy to over consume. Their low volume means you can eat more without realizing. It's about balance. I don't do well without fat, but I gain weight from eating too much fat.

Common sources of fat:

Nuts, seeds, avocado, all types of oil, butter, mayonnaise, lard, cream, and coconut oil.

There are three main kinds of fat: Polyunsaturated, Monounsaturated, and Saturated. The wisdom of the '70s declared all saturated fat artery-clogging evil, polyunsaturated the best, and the less fat in general, the better. More recently, a more complex understanding has been evolving. Saturated fat turns out to be a wonderful food, if it's the right kind of saturated fat (loosely speaking, sourced from plants (coconut oil in particular) or (grass-fed) butter rather than from animal tissue). Monounsaturated fat is the "good fat" in olive oil claimed to be the source of Mediterranean longevity. Polyunsaturated fats in their omega-3 guise are now understood to be essential but fragile, and polyunsaturated fats also include the dreaded trans fats, the most heart-unhealthy fats of all. It is wise to be informed in your choices around fats— repeatedly deep fried vegetable oil is a seriously bad idea—but our focus here is to build awareness around our experience of eating from each food group. Fats make food more palatable, and metabolize slowly, so they tend to give you a steady supply of energy for longer than any other macronutrient.

It's important for you to become aware of how different foods affect you. Pay attention to whether foods stimulate or satisfy your appetite, and how they affect your mood, mental clarity, and energy. Finding the right balance of macronutrients will help you feel satisfied with less food, and maintain your weight naturally.

It's the Foods You Eat Regularly, Not the Exceptions, that Impact You Most

Our bodies come into balance when we stop eating the foods that create an imbalance, and increase the revitalizing, nutritious foods that nourish us.

However, when we focus too much on eliminating foods, we often obsess about them. Focus on adding healthy foods into your diet, rather than obsessing over foods you think you "shouldn't" eat. When you fill up on wholesome foods, there's less room for over-indulgence.

The habits that cause poor health and weight gain are what you do regularly, not the exceptions. If you mostly ate well and enjoyed pizza and ice cream occasionally, without overdoing it, you'd probably feel great. Many of us don't realize how much we're actually eating. Or perhaps your body's changed and you can't get away with eating as much anymore. A healthy treat may be a cookie once a week, but many of us can't stop after one cookie, and we eat the whole pack, or get into a habit of eating a cookie everyday.

Sometimes it's tricky, because we think we're eating healthily. Many of my clients say things like, "I rarely eat Sugar" or "I barely eat anything at all." In some cases that may be true. Sometimes weight gain and poor health are due to genetics or unfortunate lifestyle factors like having to work the graveyard shift, but mostly it's our unhealthy habits that impact us most.

I used to think I would always be too fat no matter what I did. I thought I wasn't eating much and made good choices, which was true most of the time, but my binges negated my healthy efforts. Do you think your issues are because of your genetics or what you eat?

Breakfast Is Key

I'm sure you've heard breakfast is the most important meal of the day, but have you experimented to discover whether that's true for you?

Do you eat breakfast, or do you suppress your hunger with caffeine, thinking you'll eat less overall?

I skipped breakfast, or just ate fruit for years, which is common in people with eating disorders. I'd make myself a cup of black tea first thing in the morning. When I started to get hungry, I'd have another cup. Then I'd work out and drink water to suppress my appetite. After working out I'd have a decaf coffee and a piece of fruit, which usually suppressed my appetite until lunch. If I was hungry I'd ignore it.

I'd eat a light lunch, but by 4:00 p.m. I was ravenous. My blood Sugar dropped so low that it took large quantities of food to feel satisfied. I'd snack on healthy foods, like fruit, vegetables, grains, healthy fats, and protein, but I'd eat three times more than my body needed. If I ignored my hunger until dinner, I'd binge even more, because by that time I was famished. My hunger and binges got worse the longer I waited. I felt I had earned the right to eat because I hadn't eaten all day, but I ended up eating more than if I had eaten three meals spaced evenly throughout the day. I usually wasn't hungry the next morning, because I was still digesting the binge from the night before. I'd get caught in cycles of skipping breakfast and bingeing at night for months on end.

111

Sometimes I broke the cycle by eating breakfast, even though I wasn't hungry. I binged less frequently, made healthier choices, and ate less overall, whenever I ate breakfast. I still overate emotionally at times, but breakfast satisfied my body nutritionally, so at least I didn't crave large quantities of food later. The emotional triggers and habits of overeating were hard enough to overcome, without physical cravings.

Sometimes I broke the cycle by eating a light dinner, which was even more effective than eating breakfast after a late night binge, but it required more discipline. I'd wake up happy and hungry, looking forward to a nourishing breakfast, which set me up for success for the rest of the day. If you eat breakfast, especially when you choose the right foods for your biochemical individuality, you'll probably feel better and eat less over all.

Finding the right foods for breakfast is equally important. I've experimented extensively. I do best when I have protein and fiber for breakfast. One of my favorite breakfasts is fruit, protein, and chia seeds. I've tried gluten-free grains like millet and quinoa, oatmeal, eggs and vegetables, quiche, squash, legumes, seaweed and veggies, whole grain crepes, big breakfasts, high-fat breakfasts, low-fat breakfasts, high-carb and low-carb breakfasts, and protein-rich breakfasts.

Many experts say breakfast should be your biggest meal. I've found a balance of macronutrients in reasonable quantities works best for me. If I eat too much, I feel heavy and I'm not hungry for lunch. Eating a big breakfast sets up a similar cycle as skipping breakfast. I get hungry later in the afternoon, overeat, and skip dinner; and then I get hungry and eat again at 10:00 p.m., which makes me gain weight very quickly.

Eating the right foods in appropriate amounts sets you up for success. A healthy, energizing breakfast balances your body for the day. When you don't eat enough, eat too much, or eat refined foods like Bread, that elevate your blood Sugar quickly, your signals of hunger and satiety can go out of balance.

Mindful Piggy Playtime Breakfast Experiment

To find sustaining and energizing breakfasts for your body, let's experiment! Connect with Piggy's sensitivity and intuitive intelligence to find optimal breakfast options. Piggy intuitively knows which foods are right for you. When you wake up, take time to tune in to your body. What do you feel like eating? Are you hungry? If you're not hungry, start with something light, and experiment with eating less at night, so that you're hungry for breakfast. It may take a couple of days for your body to adjust, but you'll be thrilled with the results.

Open the fridge or pantry, and notice which foods you're drawn to. If you're in the negative expression of Piggy you may want pancakes or Bread with lots of syrup, butter, or jam. To break those habits, imagine how you'll feel when you're done eating. Do you want to feel light and energized or heavy? What will a nourishing breakfast enable you to accomplish during your day?

If you're drawn to comfort foods or you're afraid of gaining weight from eating breakfast, take a deep breath and feel your heart. Your heart can reveal what's best for

113

you. The in-between phase of changing habits may feel awkward. Connecting with why you want to change, and what you will receive from cultivating healthier habits can be very beneficial. Sometimes it's helpful to take a hot shower while you tune in to your breakfast. Feel the warm, soothing water, and the loving care of your heart as you shampoo your hair. Let the water cleanse you, so that you feel refreshed– ready for a new day. As you shower, imagine yourself eating different breakfasts, and tune into how each option would make you feel. If you don't have what you want in the house, make the next best choice, and buy what you need next time you go shopping.

Experiment with different types of whole foods. Try convenient sources of protein, like yogurt, eggs, cottage cheese, and protein powders; or fish and meat. Try whole grains like oatmeal (remembering our "whole foods" approach), quinoa, or amaranth, all of which can be found at most health food stores. Try adding fresh fruit. I suggest limiting dried fruit, because concentrated Sugars elevate your blood Sugar quickly, unless you eat small quantities. You can add fiber, like soaked or ground flax or chia seeds, to fill you up and clean you out, in addition to providing essential fatty acids. Soak a tablespoon of flax or chia seeds in four times as much water overnight to stir into your hot cereal.

Try butter, olive oil, or almond butter on a slice of wholegrain Bread to see whether you do well with carbs in the morning. Play with tweaking the amounts and balance of macronutrients until you find energizing, satiating breakfasts. Establish healthy morning routines to replace unhealthy habits. We're creatures of habit, so use it to your advantage!

Notice how you feel later in the day as you experiment with different breakfast options. Which foods give you sustained energy? Do you notice a difference in your mood and subsequent food choices, depending on what you have for breakfast?

To become aware of how different foods affect you, you may want to eat an omelet for breakfast one morning and oatmeal the next day, to determine whether protein, grain, or a combination is most satiating. For more accurate results, eat whichever breakfast you choose for three consecutive days to account for other variables. Connect with Watchdog's clarity to determine and evaluate the best options.

Water Helps You Make Healthier Choices

People often mistake thirst for hunger and end up eating when they really need water. You may want to try drinking water to see if it eases your hunger between meals. Many people are chronically dehydrated without even realizing it. They drink soda, juice, tea, or coffee, all of which can be dehydrating. It can be misleading, because you think you're hydrating your body by drinking these liquids. You may not even feel thirsty, because our bodies are amazing at adjusting to our habits, even the unhealthy ones.

Once you start drinking more water you'll feel a difference. Your body inherently wants to be healthy. It feels good to give your body what it needs. Drinking enough water is probably the most important key to optimal health. Our bodies can only be as healthy as the cleanliness of the water moving through our cells. Constipation can be caused by dehydration. Your body is smart in how it uses water, and the colon is one of the last places to get water, so if you don't drink enough you may have trouble eliminating. Not drinking enough water can make you tired and irritable. The next time you have a craving, drink water. You may lose interest in the unhealthy food, or at least you won't eat as much of it.

I'm sure you've heard that we should drink a minimum of eight glasses of water a day, which would be approximately two liters. That's a minimum for optimal health! The amount of water you need depends on how much you weigh, your activity level, climate, and how much water you lose through bodily functions, such as sweating, breathing, and even blinking your eyelids.

One good way to increase your water intake is to start your day with one or two big glasses upon waking, and carry a water bottle that holds 2 liters, to sip throughout the day. That way you don't even need to keep track. Celebrate as you drink your last sip, simply because it feels good to take care of your body.

Watchdog Mindfulness: Clearing Your Fridge

Now that you've been building a healthy foundation of whole foods, and finding a satisfying balance of macronutrients, it's time to get rid of foods that might tempt you.

Let's begin by clearing your refrigerator and cupboards. Changing habits is challenging enough without having ice cream and potatoes chips call out to you. Get rid of, or take a break from the foods that trigger unhealthy eating until your appetite comes into balance.

We're not doing this to punish or deprive you of your favorite foods. We're creating a healing environment by giving you a break from the addictive impulses that make you overeat. Trust me, throwing out addictive foods makes healthy eating so much easier. You've probably noticed that the more addictive foods you eat, the more you crave them. And if you keep them stocked in the kitchen, you're more likely to eat them than if you have to go to the store. Isn't that true?

Clearing your fridge is a great opportunity to connect with the essential qualities of Watchdog. When Watchdog decides to do something, nothing gets in the way! To connect with your strength, think of an area of your life or an activity where you're single-pointed and focused, like you did in the determination meditation in chapter three.

Think of an activity that's easy for you. I love cleaning, particularly my kitchen. You may like balancing your checkbook, organizing papers, or clearing your closet. Perhaps you like to prepare your children's school lunches. Choose something that's effortless. Imagine you're doing it right now and connect with the essential qualities you're expressing. Feel how satisfying it is to accomplish something that's important to you. Take a moment to connect with your ability to do whatever it takes to be successful to achieve your goals.

Now that you've connected with Watchdog's essential qualities by imagining an activity you enjoy, clear out your fridge. Continue connecting with your strengths as you open your fridge and pull out all your temptations. Look inside the meat drawers, the door, and the freezer. Clear the top shelves, the lower shelves, and all the shelves in between. Get rid of all the items Piggy's tucked away between vegetables, or behind milk cartons. Don't forget any of Piggy's special hiding places.

When you're done with the fridge, throw out Piggy's secret stashes from your cupboards, purse, and car. Be thorough and honest with yourself about which foods might trigger your desire for more. Connect with Watchdog's clarity and strength as you take action to make healthy eating a priority.

Softly Saying Goodbye

If you're not ready to throw food out that's okay. If Piggy's still too attached to certain foods, pace yourself. At times I've needed to enjoy foods slowly, while saying goodbye, before I was ready to let go of them. I'd stand in front of the fridge eating, or make multiple trips to the kitchen, until I finished every morsel. Piggy needed time to say goodbye.

If you're not ready to let go of certain foods, give yourself permission to enjoy them without guilt or shame. Softly say goodbye, as you savor each bite. This might be your phase of "bringing love to bingeing." I needed to embrace Piggy for a while before I was able to throw food out or not buy it. You may be tired of overeating and ready to throw things out now. Great! Otherwise, gently say goodbye for now.

You can also give food away. You may find it helpful to lock things up. You could give the key to your partner, a family member, or roommate, and ask them to give you one portion at a time. Do what's most supportive. Your readiness to change is the key. It's important to respect yourself by honoring where you are. Ironically, the charge that keeps us attached to food dissolves when we acknowledge and relax with being attached. Have you ever noticed that soon after you stopped wanting something, it came? Forcing ourselves to change usually isn't effective or enjoyable long-term. Acceptance, and being at peace with things as they are is transformative.

If you're ready for the challenge, go for it! Leave the clean-plate club and join the body-wisdom club. Feel the relief as you get rid of your unhealthy temptations, so that you don't get tested repeatedly. Give yourself a break from saying things like, "Maybe I'll just have a little" but then a little can turn into a lot. Throwing food out can save pounds from settling on your belly, hips, and thighs!

Chapter Five

Smart Choices at the Grocery Store

Many of our choices begin at the grocery store. Being mindful while shopping can be enough to transform your body. If you make excellent choices at the grocery store you don't need to torture yourself with temptations at home. Make choices in a split second, instead of testing yourself repeatedly.

Maitri's Success Story

I sat in my car and connected with my heart to center myself before I went into the store. I had made a list and only bought what was on my list. I didn't buy any chocolate or biscuits. I was accustomed to have tea and biscuits every afternoon from growing up in Australia. If I had bought them I surely would have eaten them. I'm happy I spent time thinking about whether I was going to buy the sweets before I went in. The chocolate and biscuits still called out to me, but I was prepared. I heard Tarika's voice in my head saying: "You can pass by items you crave and find healthy, satisfying alternatives." I bought a bag of sweet, juicy pears instead, and thoroughly enjoyed them with my afternoon tea.

Maitri, Australia

Whether you are aware of it or not, the items you grab at the grocery store can determine whether you fit into your jeans.

Aren't you more likely to eat ice cream when it's in the freezer? How often do you make special trips to the grocery store when you have a craving, especially when it's late at night? I'm guessing it depends on how strong your cravings are, but there are likely times you let cravings pass, or eat what's available, because you don't feel like going out.

This chapter teaches you how to make healthy, smart choices at the grocery store, as that's where many of your choices begin. If you don't buy it, you're less likely to eat it, aren't you? At the grocery store you can make decisions in a split second, whereas when you have trigger foods in the house, you may need to resist temptations dozens of times. I find it much easier to walk past the cookie aisle, and be done with it.

When your heart guides your choices, you intuitively know what to buy, and can easily pass by items that may trigger unhealthy eating.

The meditative practices in this chapter bring awareness to different aspects of shopping, by breaking it down into simple steps so that you can make healthy choices every time you shop. You can start with one, or try them all to see which ones are helpful. If some of them don't work for you, experiment to find your own ways to make healthy choices, consistently.

I turned grocery shopping into a spiritual classroom when I realized that every time I shopped I gained weight. I'd eat all my "treats" within a couple of days, while neglecting healthy proteins and vegetables. I'd eat bags of chips, hunks of cheese, or several protein bars in one sitting, especially when I was premenstrual. I'd say things to myself like, "Now that you've started you might as well finish, because you're going on a diet tomorrow." Do you have a tendency to go "all the way" once you've started making poor choices? "Tomorrow" usually took several weeks, or months to come, until Watchdog finally forced me to comply. After losing a few pounds, less than what I'd gained, Piggy would mindlessly wander through the isles of Whole Foods, sneaking whatever she could past Watchdog.

Don't be fooled by snacks and treats at health food stores! Even though they're generally better for you, Sugar, fat, flour, and salt, in whatever form, especially combined, can easily trigger addictive eating and weight gain.

Piggy had a tendency to buy more than I needed. Sometimes she'd buy sale items, but instead of saving money I just ate more. Do you ever stock up, or buy items you don't need and end up eating just because they're there, when you'd actually prefer something else? Becoming aware of my shopping habits enabled me to change them, so now I mostly buy what I need and really want. I swiftly pass by trigger foods, and when I accidently grab something that isn't healthy for me, sometimes with the excuse, "I'm buying it for someone else," I put it back. Even though I love to be generous, I've often eaten those so-called food gifts on my way home.

Do you ever buy food for your kids, or loved ones and end up eating it? I'd also buy items thinking there can't be harm in eating one portion, but then I'd eat the whole thing.

Have you ever eaten a few handfuls of chips, but couldn't stop yourself from going back for more, repeatedly until you finished them? When I really wanted something that would likely trigger my desire for more, like nuts, dark Chocolate, or raw goat cheese, I bought one or two portions at a time. I learned to allow Piggy pleasure, while connecting with Watchdog 's clarity to determine how much, and which treats to buy. Piggy sometimes obsessed over foods I'd lost my taste for, or that someone one close to me ate, but then when I ate them I'd realize I wasn't enjoying them as much as I thought I would.

Do you ever buy things that you used to love, or thought you wanted, but then realized they're not nearly as good as you'd remembered, or imagined? Making conscious choices at the grocery store, instead of falling victim to the imbalances of Piggy and Watchdog will likely transform your body, especially if you eat a high percentage of your meals at home. However, as you know, you can't always control the foods you have at home when you live with others, particularly kids.

When I lived with my boyfriend and his two daughters, there was always Bread, cereal, cheese, cookies, Chocolate, ice cream, chips, nuts, and candy in the house. In some ways it's more challenging to make healthy choices when everyone around you is eating whatever they want, but in my experience living alone can be equally, if not more challenging. I rarely pig out in front others, yet when I'm alone my feeling of loneliness can drive Piggy to eat large quantities into the wee hours of the night.

Are you more of a sneak eater, or do you tend to overeat with others? Be careful not to make too many excuses for yourself. There will likely be temptations, no matter where you go. The key is to use your creative intelligence to respond to situations as they arise. You can ask your family or housemates to hide your trigger foods, or inspire them to eat healthily with you. Several years ago, before I realized that restrictive eating led me to binge, I decided to go on a raw-food cleanse. I was working out intensely every day, taking a ski conditioning class five days a week, and running and weightlifting afterwards. I got "high" from the endorphins of exercise and hunger.

Watchdog was finally winning! YAY. I had almost reached my goal weight by not eating and exercising for several hours a day, until I went to the grocery store. I knew I couldn't sustain myself on dry salad for too much longer, so I decided to buy the ingredients to make sprouted nut dishes. I was talking to my friend Gloria on the phone, wandering through Trader Joes, grabbing big bags of almonds, cashews, and raisins. I had good intentions, but when I got home Piggy started frantically devouring handfuls of each. I ate about two thirds of each bag that night, close to 10,000 calories! I spent hours tossing and turning with the worst bellyache of my life!

If I could have vomited I probably would have. Thankfully that's never worked for me. If you do struggle with bulimia please seek help. Even though it's a challenging issue and slow process, I've had great success with my clients, and would gladly help you.

After several more days of compulsively eating raw food I couldn't believe what I saw. I was doing lunges in front of the mirror and it seemed like my hips and butt had quadrupled in size. That was the fastest weight gain

I've ever experienced, even faster than my fifty-five pound gain in Sedona, and it all started at the grocery store!

Identifying Your Shopping Habits

Now lets practice identifying imbalanced characteristics of Piggy and Watchdog shoppers, to make it easy for you to become aware of your shopping tendencies. Remember, becoming mindful of your habits is the first step to changing them.

Piggy Shopping Tendencies

- Buys more than you need, or sale items to "save money" or "just in case".
- Buys everything that looks good, like three kinds of cheese, or several treats instead of one or two.
- Buys large quantities.
- Chooses comfort foods, like salty snacks, or sweet treats, over protein, whole grains, and vegetables.
- Struggles with decisions, and sometimes picks up and puts back the same item several times.
- Samples, or nibbles on things before you get to the register.
- Impulsive: doesn't consider what you need, or what's on your grocery list (if you have one). Even when you're shopping for a recipe you often buy additional items.
- Talks on the phone, or to people, and easily gets distracted.
- Gets influenced by others, samples, the sight or smell of foods, or is driven by cravings.
- Have memories and associations with certain foods, and buys them even though they may not be healthy for you.
- Buys foods for others, or as a "gift" but ends up eating them.

Watchdog Shopping Tendencies

- Buys the cheapest items.
- Only buys what you need, and often a little less.
- Focuses on a list, and zooms past unnecessary items.
- Too quick to make decisions, and oversees items you may have needed or wanted.
- Denies you of your favorite foods, "you don't need that", or "it's fattening".
- Analyzes and buys items for their value, or caloric and nutritional content, rather than buying what you want.
- Negotiates, "Ok, you can have a little treat if you must, but then you can't have anything else, or you'll have to make up for it later."
- Ignores hunger pangs and makes you wait until your next meal, instead of buying a snack and eating when you're hungry.
- Punishes you if you've been eating "too much" by buying less.

Mark the tendencies you recognize in yourself from both lists. You may find that you have a combination of Piggy and Watchdog shopping traits, you may lean to one side, or you might switch back and forth depending on what you're going through. You may have a mixture. I've slightly exaggerated them to make it clear. Even if you experience them to a lesser degree mark them anyway. If you don't identify with any make your own list, or take note of shopping behaviors as you become aware of them.

Next Time You Go Shopping

You may want to scan the lists above before you go shopping, to become more alert. When you recognize a tendency while shopping, pause for a moment and take a deep breath. Connect with your heart to give space to your thoughts, emotions, and impulses. You can ask your heart, "Will I love myself if I buy, and most likely, eat this?"

The other day I was about to buy a scoop of dark Chocolate almonds, when I realized that I wanted to eat the whole scoop before I even put them in the bag. I saw myself compulsively eating them before I even got to the register and devouring the rest on my way home. I felt the urgency of desire in my body. I decided not to buy them, and walked away.

That's a clear example of how my intuitive wisdom revealed what was right for me. I had a vision of myself compulsively eating, felt the energy of craving, and realized that Chocolate was going to trigger me. If I had felt a loving response, or sensed that I would have been able to enjoy a handful without it triggering me, no problem. That clearly wasn't the case.

Remember, you receive your body wisdom through the intuition of your heart. It can come through any, or all of your senses. So pay attention to how you feel when you reach for certain foods, whether they're visually appealing, or whether you receive a message from your body intuition as to what it needs.

Mindful Grocery Shopping

Now that you've identified some of your shopping tendencies, and understand the importance of tuning into your body intuition to make choices that are right for you, I'm going to share the meditative practices that helped me shop without getting taken over by impulsive habits and buying indulgences.

Make a List Before You Go Shopping

Deciding what you're going to buy before you go is an easy way to minimize unhealthy choices. Piggy and Watchdog's conflicting opinions, debating about which foods to buy, can be disconcerting. We typically try to ignore their overwhelming chatter, but in doing so, we disconnect from our intuitive wisdom. We might imprudently follow whichever voice is strongest, without tuning into our bodies.

Making lists and going shopping are both excellent opportunities to connect with your body intuition, like we did in chapter three. You may want to practice that meditation again, because your body intuition is a vital key to buying, and consequently eating, what's right for you.

Let's get practical

Mindful Watchdog Activity: Connecting With Your Body Intuition

As You Make a Grocery List

First take a moment to feel your heart, so that you can receive your body intuition. Then look in your fridge and cupboards, and take time to consider what you're in the mood for. Seeing certain items might inspire you to make a dish you haven't made in a while.

Make a list and tune into the items on your list. Are any of them likely to trigger addictive eating, or call out to you saying: "Eat me, eat me"? Will it be easy for you to stop after one portion, or do you have a history of overeating that food? Is a few seconds of pleasure worth the struggle? Put a question mark next to any items you're weary of, and cross off the items you're likely to overeat. It's important to be honest with yourself and respect where you are. Don't buy foods that are likely to tempt you, unless you feel comfortable eating them. Now tune into your "questionable" items. As you look at each item, ask your body wisdom: "How will I feel if I eat this?" Receive the answer inside your heart.

Remember your intuition communicates with you through your senses; be open to receive its messages in whatever ways they come to you. You may see yourself overeating an item, or hear a voice saying "no that doesn't feel good". When you imagine yourself eating your "questionable" foods notice whether you feel tense, or energized.

You'll most likely cross off most your questionable items, as it becomes clear how they might affect you. If you really want some of your old trigger-food-favorites, consider the balance of eating for health and pleasure, to determine where you are on the continuum. I think a balanced relationship with food can include treats in reasonable quantities. Decide which treats, and how much you're going to buy, and write them down. If you're following a healthy eating plan, only buy the items on your food plan and try this exercise at a later time.

Please be patient with yourself and don't worry if you accidently buy trigger foods. You'll become more attuned to your intuitive wisdom overtime, especially when you pay attention to what happens when you buy, and then eat, your "questionable" foods.

The real test comes when you have them at home. If you end up overeating certain foods, that information will help you make a better choice next time. You can choose not to buy that item, even if you want it. You can take a break from it, or you can buy one or two portions at a time. I encourage you to find healthier alternatives to your comfort foods that satisfy you without triggering a desire for more. For example, I switched from butter to coconut oil, which was equally satisfying, but not as addictive. I got totally into locally fresh pressed organic olive oil for a while, and now I've found a balance between different sources of healthy fats.

Sometimes you need to allow yourself your "forbidden" foods for a while until they become neutral before you can say goodbye, or enjoy them in moderation. I ate an alarming amount of butter before I understood that the more I ate, the more I wanted, and that butter would never fulfill me. Now I see it for what it is- food, not love, and I enjoy it occasionally when I go out, but I haven't craved it in years. It's not an issue anymore.

Go grocery shopping and only buy what's on your list, unless you feel intuitively drawn to something. It's best to go when you're not hungry, because it's easier to remain centered. If your old favorites temporarily distract you, come back to your list, and move on. If they keep beckoning you, try standing in front of them for a moment and asking yourself, "If I eat this will I feel satisfied, or will I crave more?" Once you receive your intuitive wisdom, follow it! The gentle whispers of your intuition will become loud and clear the more you listen to them.

Following Your Body Intuition While Grocery

Shopping Meditation

This is another excellent meditative practice that you can either use in addition to, or instead of the grocery list meditation. If you don't like planning and making lists, this might be perfect for you.

❖ Before you go into the store, take a few moments to connect with your heart. In your heart you naturally connect to your body intuition. Your body will "tell" you what it needs.

❖ Take a deep breath, and feel your heart. Come into the moment through your senses, by noticing the sounds around you. Perhaps you hear the voices of Watchdog and Piggy denying, or begging you for certain foods.

❖ As you walk into the store continue to feel your heart, and imagine that your eyes are connected to your heart. As you look at different foods tune into your body. Some foods might seem brighter as you feel an expansion inside, and other foods might look unappealing, making you contract. Trust your instincts, and select the foods that "sing" to you.

❖ When you're uncertain of an item, pause, and ask yourself: "Will I love myself if I eat this?" This question will naturally evoke your body intuition. Receive the answer and make an empowering choice.

Putting Items Back While Standing in the Checkout Line

If you have a habit of stocking up and buying more than you need this is an excellent way to break it. Instead of buying several types of lettuce, cheese, or whatever you buy, challenge yourself to choose one. It's also a perfect backup plan for when Piggy tries to trick you into buying something you don't need, even after you've made a list and connected with your body intuition.

This is especially effective for kinesthetic (feeling) types, like myself, and many of us who like to eat. Sometimes tuning into the items on your list isn't enough, but waiting in line gives you ample time to hold questionable items in your hands, and feel whether they would trigger unhealthy eating.

You may need to let Piggy grab your favorites for a while, instead of fighting with yourself or feeling ashamed for wanting them. When you allow your desire and you see that buying them will likely trigger overeating, it becomes easier to let them go. Not buying foods that might make you suffer unnecessarily is the most loving choice you could make.

You can also look at the items in your basket before you get to the register, and compare them to your list, if you made one, to determine whether you overbought, or forgot something. If you're hesitant about an item, don't buy it! I've found my hesitation usually comes from my intuitive wisdom– a deeper sense that it's likely to trigger unhealthy eating.

Mindful Watchdog Activity: If You Accidently Grab Something, Put It Back Meditation

- ❖ Before you get to the register connect with one of Watchdog's essential qualities, like power, clarity, or strength. Choose whichever one appeals to you.
- ❖ Take a deep breath, allowing it to fill your chest and open your heart. In your heart you can easily connect with Watchdog's essential qualities. Feel the quality you chose inside, like a bright sun in the center of your belly, radiating from deep within, filling your whole body.
- ❖ Connect with your body intuition again, allowing your eyes to become soft and receptive– like windows to your heart. As you look at the foods in your basket, notice whether you're uncertain about any of them.
- ❖ Put back, or politely hand over any of Piggy's old favorites, or surplus. Don't worry about what others think. Do this for yourself!

You can also come up with your own experiment. Ask yourself, what would minimize temptations at home? Your intuitive wisdom is the most powerful, and creative healer.

Smart Choices at the Grocery Store Summary

Connect with your body intuition and make a list before you go shopping. Tune into the items on your list and cross off any items you're likely to overeat. If you really want something, decide how much you're going to buy and write it down. Try not to go shopping when you're hungry, or emotionally triggered, and only buy the items on your list, unless your intuitive wisdom tells you otherwise.

If Piggy sneaks something into your basket, put it back, or politely hand it over to the cashier. Remember, if you accidently buy something that isn't right for you it's never too late to throw it, or the rest of it away.

Nutrition Tip: 1. Protein

"Most Americans eat more protein than they need, so a percentage Daily Value is not required on food labels. Eat moderate portions of lean meat, poultry, fish, eggs, low-fat milk, yogurt and cheese, plus beans, peanut butter and nuts."

Pros of protein:

The benefit of following a high protein diet, in terms of weight loss is that your body switches from burning carbohydrates as fuel to burning your own body fat. This produces ketones, which tend to suppress your appetite.

Cons of protein:

As carbohydrates are replaced by protein, you get less of the vital nutrients they contain like fiber, vitamins, antioxidants and phyto nutrients that can prevent disease. Animal protein sources tend to be high in saturated fats, which can increase the risk of certain diseases.

Eat Right- Academy of Nutrition and Diabetics
http://www.eatright.org/resource/food/nutrition/nutrition-facts-and-food-labels/the-basics-of-the-nutrition-facts-panel
WebMD
http://www.webmd.com/men/features/benefits-protein?page=2

Chapter Six

Cooking with Love

If you had healthy, delicious satiating foods available at all times, what would you choose? You can transform cooking into a mindful, creative, fun and engaging activity. Home cooked meals can be seriously satisfying.

Annette's Success Story

"I'm not on a diet. I try to eat when I'm hungry and stop when I'm full. I mostly eat what's good for my body. I've been experimenting with this for a while, and it works well when I'm relaxed and have time, but when I'm busy I lose it.

Cooking with Love was the missing link. It made it easier to prepare food. I used to feel like cooking was another chore, on my already-too-busy schedule. Now I enjoy looking in the fridge, shopping, and preparing food in the evening for the next day."

"If I connect to the enjoyment while cooking I don't feel so much need anymore to treat myself with all the sweat and fattening stuff that's around."

Annette H., Germany

Cooking is one of the easiest times to meditate. Holding ingredients in your hands, peeling onions, or snapping off the tips of green beans is a perfect time to feel your heart. Your heart is the bridge to your body intuition. Because cooking is such a rich, sensory hands-

138

on experience it's easy to develop a deeper connection with food, and feel how your body responds. The sensation of running water as you wash produce, and the rhythmic motion of chopping vegetables can engage, and open all of your senses. Becoming aware of your senses brings you into the moment.

Cooking can be almost as sensuous as eating, especially when you take time to smell the delicious aromas, savoring little tastes until you find the perfect blend of flavors to make you moan with pleasure. Apart from eating, cooking allows you to melt and merge with food more easily than the other food situations. We long to become one with food. Eating and cooking gives us that opportunity multiple times a day!

Cooking is the ultimate opportunity to tune into how different foods affect you; so that you can prepare them exactly the way you want. You have the most control over what you eat, and the least amount of compromise out of all the food situations. Even if you're cooking for family or friends, and need to consider their needs and preferences, you can use your creativity to find healthy ways to take everyone into account. You can choose how much oil to use, select your favorite ingredients, and experiment with new cooking styles. Perhaps you're in the mood for cheese instead of nuts, or extra olives, for example. Restaurant and premade foods generally prioritize taste over nutrition, whereas when you cook you can easily turn simple ingredients into exquisite wholesome meals.

Have you ever tasted anything better than a carefully prepared home-cooked meal? You can taste the love and care, can't you? Sometimes you can even feel your body thanking you for the nourishment, particularly from slow cooking methods that allow foods to marinate in their own juices for hours. The delicate release of flavors fusing together from high quality ingredients puts packaged foods to shame. The family and cultural traditions that get passed on through cooking, and the delectable simplicity of steamed vegetables can't be replaced by anything!

Cooking builds a healthy foundation. It's one of the most gratifying food situations, because a little effort can produce outstanding results. To be able to fine tune flavors, textures, and nutritional value to your liking so precisely, makes food so much more satisfying. Home cooked meals sensitize your taste buds, so you begin to prefer, and even crave nature's bountiful resources. Once you get used to the benefits of eating simply, even though you might enjoy richer foods on occasion, you'll likely look forward to your own cooking.

Perhaps you already enjoy cooking, or maybe this is the most challenging situation of all. We all have different strengths and weaknesses that either support or undermine our ability to eat healthily. These meditative practices build upon your strengths, so that you can easily overcome the challenges that get in the way of home-cooked meals.

If you rarely have time to cook, or feel insecure about cooking, you may want to invite a friend over who enjoys cooking, participate in a cooking class, or watch a cooking show, in addition to these meditative practices and the Cooking with Love guided meditation. It's important to connect with your heart while cooking, as your heart dissolves resistance and insecurities that may be in the way of your creativity. Start with simple meals, and gradually build upon your strengths until you're ready to try more elaborate recipes.

Give yourself permission to make mistakes. I taught myself to cook through trial and error. Sometimes I made fabulous concoctions, and once in a while I threw things out. Following recipes may have been easier, but Piggy wouldn't have had as much fun. I also wouldn't have felt the same level of accomplishment.

If you live in a metropolitan area and you need to rely on restaurants and takeout meals, or you travel for work, don't worry. I'll help you make healthy choices regardless of your schedule in the chapter on Eating Healthily in Social Situations. I encourage you to practice connecting with your loving care, even if you only prepare simple snacks, wash an apple, or pour yourself a glass of water. Each time you connect with love, it's nourishing, and it grows so that it's available when you need it. Loving care is an essential ingredient to making healthy choices, so use every opportunity you can to connect with the love inside your heart. Love transforms your body, and literally every aspect of your life.

These meditations can unleash your culinary genius. It's remarkable when you experience infinite sources of creativity that produce satisfying meals again, and again, and again! Your awareness can continually, and exponentially expand in your very own kitchen! What was once a place of unhealthy eating, followed by guilt and shame, can become a healing sanctuary.

Here's a quote I came across while studying nutrition that clearly illustrates the importance of your internal state while cooking.

"If a woman could see the sparks of light going forth from her fingertips when she is cooking and the substance of light that goes into the food she handles, she would be amazed to see how much of herself she charges into the meals that she prepares for her family and friends.

It is one of the most important and least understood activities of life that the radiation and feeling that go into the preparation of food affect everyone who partakes of it, and this activity should be unhurried, peaceful and happy." [1]

What gets in the way of you making healthy meals deliciously pleasurable?

Identifying your cooking tendencies can alert you to ways you can improve. Mark the Piggy and Watchdog tendencies you resonate with from the lists below and add anything else that prevents you from having an abundance of healthy, delicious food available at all times.

Piggy Cooking Tendencies

- I'm often too lazy or tired to cook, so I order takeout, have cereal or toast, or heat up packaged foods.

———————————————

- Sometimes I munch on snacks and lose my appetite before I even have time to consider what to make.
- I can get so tempted by my own delicious creations, that I taste them repeatedly, and occasionally need to make a new batch.
- I often get hungry and impatient, and end up throwing something together that isn't satisfying, so I keep eating, or go back into the kitchen for another course, or helping.
- Low blood Sugar levels make me ravenous, "I'm going to starve to death if I don't eat now", which disrupts my ability to tune into what I need, so I make poor choices.
- I can get carried away, thinking "the richer the better", or I accidently over-salt or over-spice a dish to the point where the intensity and complexity of too many flavors become overpowering.
- I feel insecure and overwhelmed by the thought of cooking, so I don't even try.

Watchdog's Cooking Tendencies

- I sometimes eat the same thing over and over again, because I can't think of what else to make.
- I tend to follow recipes closely, but I don't know how to adjust them to my needs and preferences.
- I'm afraid of using too much oil, salt, or spice, so my cooking can be bland and monotonous.
- Sometimes I wonder whether small amounts of elaborate ingredients like wholegrain flour, a sprinkle of cheese, nuts, or natural sweeteners might make a dish more satisfying, but I'm afraid of gaining weight, so I don't even try.
- "I don't have time to cook, I'm too busy".
- Cooking is a chore, another thing on my to-do-list.
- I rather not cook because I think that if there's too much food around I'll eat more.

It's not important whether you're more of a Watchdog or Piggy cook. As you can see they both have their strengths and weaknesses. What's important is that you recognize, and honor your nature. Becoming aware of who is cooking can help you determine whether your cooking style produces satisfactory results. If Piggy and Watchdog already dance beautifully in the kitchen, great! You can still use cooking as a time to feel your heart and connect with your body, because it will help you in other food situations.

Creating Outstanding Meals

Now that you've identified some of your imbalances, look at the lists below and choose a Piggy or Watchdog cooking strength you feel drawn toward. You can also use the list to inspire you to come up with your own intentions. These cooking strengths key you into your essential qualities, making it easier and more enjoyable to make delicious, satisfying meals.

Setting intentions can help you develop yourself in new ways. Once you've identified how you want to expand and enrich your cooking experience, your intuitive intelligence will find ways to manifest it. If you lean towards Piggy cooking tendencies, you may want to choose Watchdog strength, but not necessarily.

I'm more of a Piggy cook by nature. As I connected to my joy and creativity I found balance, and came in touch with Piggy's true power in the kitchen. Even though my cooking style can be elaborate and innovative in flavor, I use simple ingredients and healthy cooking methods.

Piggy Cooking Strengths

- I want to connect with loving care, so that my cooking deeply nourishes others, and myself physically and emotionally.
- I want to connect with creativity and spontaneity, so that I can open my fridge and make outstanding meals within minutes from whatever's available.
- I want to connect with flexibility and care, so that I can tweak recipes to make my loved ones happy by catering to their preferences and needs.
- I want to connect with my intuitive intelligence, so that I can explore and find healthier ways of cooking without compromising flavor and texture.
- I want to connect with boundless creativity to create endless variety, so that I don't get board of healthy food.

Watchdog Cooking Strengths

- I want to become attuned to my body's needs, so that I can maintain balance between eating for health and pleasure.
- I want to plan and prepare my meals, or follow a food plan without being seduced by unhealthy temptations.
- I want to time each dish so that everything's cooked to perfection, and served hot and fresh.

146

- I want to connect with discipline so that I can wait until mealtimes, and eat well throughout the day, so that I don't overeat.
- I want to be more organized in the kitchen, so that I have easy access to all the right ingredients.
- I want to be focused, so that I can complete meals without getting distracted.
- I want to connect with order and put things away as I cook, so that I don't get overwhelmed with piles of dishes.
- I want to connect with patience, so that I can utilize slower cooking methods.
- I want to be more precise in following recipes, by weighing and measuring ingredients instead of eyeballing it, so that I can replicate my favorite dishes.
- I want to taste my dishes to determine what they need, and add a little flavor at a time to avoid ruining them with too much of an ingredient.

Now that you've chosen one or two essential elements to enhance your cooking, let's practice the Connecting with Loving Care While Cooking meditation.

Connecting with Loving Care While Cooking teaches you how to connect with love and creativity, so that you can create wholesome meals effortlessly, and consistently. When you eat foods prepared in this manner, you're nourishing your body with love. Love releases excess weight and heaviness. Love is fulfilling, and love opens the door to a rainbow of Piggy and Watchdog cooking strengths.

Connecting with Loving Care While Cooking brings you into the moment, where old habits and imbalanced cooking tendencies subside. Habits, like habitually tasting food until you've eaten an entire meal, or using more butter than you need, can easily be replaced by healthier ways of cooking. Becoming present to the moment is like turning on the light inside; darkness instantly disappears.

Connecting with Loving Care While Cooking Meditation

❖ Before you start cooking, place your hands on your heart center. Feel your heart, allowing the touch of your hands to take you deep inside. In your heart you naturally connect with qualities of loving care. Feel this. Let it expand and flow into your shoulders, down your arms, and into your hands.

❖ Feel the warmth and energy of your heart flow through your hands as you wash and chop vegetables, stir soups and stews, and toss your meats and vegetables in the oven. Infusing your food with love.

❖ Let your body tell you which types of proteins, whole grains, vegetables, fruits, or fats you need to create a balanced, pleasurable meal. Connect with your creativity to try new combinations of herbs and spices, so that each meal nourishes you deeply.

148

A Culmination of Watchdog and Piggy Strengths:

Creating a System That Works

Now that you've identified the ways in which you'd like to improve, and learned to infuse your food with the tastiest ingredient–love, it's time to get cooking! To create a system it's easiest to begin with one meal, or cooking strategy at a time. Experiment with the most appealing cooking activities listed below, or come up with your own, to develop your own rhythm.

I began by making nourishing variations of lean proteins, vegetables, and salad for lunch every day. Then I focused on making a smoothie for breakfast, a green juice, and then several months later, I tackled dinner. Cooking created the foundation for my new way of eating. I maintained my weight because I began to enjoy my healthy meals more than anything else!

Once I established a foundation of healthy cooking, and eating, there was room for extras like wine, nuts, Chocolate, and weekly dining. I didn't need to skip meals or over-exercise to make up for it. In fact I realized that having my next meal, even if I wasn't as hungry, kept me from gaining weight. Skipping meals usually started a roller coaster of unstable blood Sugar, cravings, and addictive eating. Consistent meals enabled me to eat less because I didn't feel ravenous or deprived.

Mindful Watchdog Activity: Preparing Meals in Advance

I often listen to thought-provoking, educational, or spiritual lectures as I plan and prepare my meals for the day. I start by making a green juice or smoothie. I prewash, chop, and grate veggies so that I can make

149

scrumptious salads within minutes at any given time. I prepare enough protein and vegetables for two or three lunches at a time. I plan, or prepare things for dinner, so that it's quick and easy when I get home. I've established an effective system that guarantees delicious nourishment at every meal.

Although I never used to cook and didn't even know how, it's become one of my favorite activities. When I have a craving and I have a fridge full of the finest fixings for a salad, and a variety of mouthwatering dishes, I rarely go for unhealthy foods. There have been countless times I would have binged if I hadn't prepared healthy meals.

Establishing routines and getting into a rhythm of healthy food preparation helps you break unhealthy habits. We're creatures of habit. Use this to your advantage by creating healthy ones! Your heart will intuitively find creative strategies to form a system that makes healthy eating effortless.

Mindful Piggy Playtime

Let's Get Cooking!

Here is some Piggy mindfulness cooking suggestions to get you started. Choose one that entices you. I recommend choosing one new cooking habit and doing it regularly, until it becomes routine. When you focus on one health ritual at a time, a foundation of healthy habits naturally evolves into a new way of eating.

You may want to listen to music, audio books, podcasts, YouTube videos, or watch TV as you cook.

Find ways to make it interesting, so that cooking becomes a creative activity instead of a chore.

Yummy Smoothies

Smoothies are a quick, easy, and inexpensive way to get nutritious sustenance. All you need is a blender! You can make one for breakfast, or take it to work in a mason jar to sip throughout the day. It's the easiest way to keep your blood Sugar stable, giving you consistent energy, while keeping cravings at bay.

I've simplified my approach to making smoothies for you. I start with a base: protein powder, dairy, nuts, or seeds. Then I add fresh or frozen fruit, fiber, and I go in cycles with green food supplements, which add astounding nutritional punch and flavor.

I'm going to begin by going into the nutritional value of the three types of ingredients I use as a base. Then I'll provide you with sample recipes, and a table of ingredients, so that you can create your own concoctions. That should send you off to the races with inspiration and creativity. Smoothies can help you lose and maintain your weight without feeling hungry.

Protein Powder

Protein powders are one of the few processed foods I eat. I've found they work well for most people, especially if you do well with protein in the morning, but can't tolerate much dairy, nuts, or seeds. Out of all the types of protein powders I've tried I like brown rice, or raw sprouted protein powders best. Whey can be an excellent option if you tolerate dairy well. It's best to get

151

whey from grass-fed, hormone-free cows. Some people do well with hemp or pea protein.

Soy protein is inexpensive, buts it's a common allergen, so it tends to be problematic for certain individuals. It's highly processed and usually genetically modified. It affects hormones, and the research on the health benefits or risks of eating soy, related to cancer in particular, is mixed and inconclusive. I limit my consumption of soy for when I need a quick and easy protein for dinner, like tempeh. I tend to get a stuffy nose from tofu (even sprouted varieties), and I get bloated and gassy. I over consumed soy as a vegetarian, which is likely why I became sensitive to it. Soy is added to numerous products, which is likely contributing to the increasing number of people with soy sensitivities. We often become sensitive to foods we over-consume.

Egg white protein powders are another option, although eggs are also a common allergen, but not as common as soy and dairy sensitivities. I'll cover common food allergens in Satisfying Cravings, so that you can identify your food sensitivities. They're often the cause of cravings, addictive eating, and weight gain, among other things. I recommend trying several protein powders, while paying attention to your body until you find one you like.

Greens, and Green Food Supplements

You can add any type of green vegetable to a smoothie, particularly dark leafy and salad greens. Once you get accustomed to greens, you'll likely crave them! They're so deliciously satisfying. When I go too long without them I yearn for kale salad, and almost always choose it over pizza.

Green food supplements are particularly nutritious and detoxifying. They're a great source of protein for vegetarians, when fresh vegetables aren't enough. They're generally made from a variety of fruits and vegetables, and freeze dried grasses and seaweed such as alfalfa, barley, wheatgrass, blue green algae, Spirulina, and chlorella.

There are a variety of powdered and capsule forms on the market. My favorite brands in powdered form (I absolutely love the taste and wouldn't waste it on capsules) are Perfect Food Raw or Super Green Formula from Garden of Life, and ProGreens.

Green food powders are an abundant source of anti-oxidants, co-nutrients, enzymes, vitamins, minerals, and amino acids. Greens are alkalizing, detoxifying, and energizing. Cravings can stem from acidic body chemistry. Adding greens in any form can cut cravings, not to mention the incredible plethora of phytonutrients and their anti-carcinogenic properties.

I believe greens, protein, and fibers are key to health. When I get off track and focus on greens, protein, and fiber I feel better within a day or two.

Greens help you lose weight and make you feel great! Greens are a powerful antidepressant, particularly wheatgrass. It may be because wheatgrass is full of amino acids, but I think it also contains many vital nutrients that science hasn't even identified. Amino acid deficiencies have been linked to numerous imbalances like depression, mood swings, cravings, lack of focus, and sleep apnea, among many others.

Some people are allergic or sensitive to certain grasses and micro-greens. Pay attention to your body. If you notice any adverse symptoms stop taking the supplement and focus on fresh vegetables. It can be challenging to identify which ingredients you're sensitive to, because most green foods contain a variety of grasses and seaweeds.

Perfect Food Raw is less allergenic because it's made from vegetables, whereas grasses tend to be more allergenic. If you know or discover that you're sensitive to any of them skip green food powders altogether. You can add fresh greens to your smoothies, which is what I do most of the time, especially now that I eat animal protein and don't need the extra protein. I also drink a green juice and take a multivitamin daily, so I don't need the extra nutrition anymore, but if you do, green food supplements are excellent.

Fiber

Fiber is the secret to satiety, regularity, and very beneficial for weight loss! I don't go a day without eating a substantial amount of fiber. You can easily add ground flax or chia seeds to smoothies, yogurt, grains, and homemade crackers to increase your fiber intake. Make sure you soak or grind them and drink plenty of water. They're mucilaginous so they're excellent for the colon. They absorb a ton of water, so if you don't drink enough, you can get very constipated. I recommend starting with one teaspoon and gradually increasing to one or two tablespoons a day. You may get a little gassy while your body adjusts, but it will pass.

154

Drinking enough water and increasing your fiber intake slowly is critical! If you don't drink enough water, or increase fiber too quickly you can get totally backed up. I think that's one of the worst things ever. Without going into this too deeply, an essential sign of health is having an effortless bowel movement everyday. If that's not the case, lets talk! Seriously.

Psyllium husk can also be a great way to increase your fiber intake. It's a little more aggressive than flax and chia seeds, so if you're sensitive stick with the ground seeds. Psyllium husk is best for short periods of time while cleansing, losing weight, or to get things moving. Pay attention to your body, and stop immediately if you experience bloating or irritation. Drink one teaspoon in eight ounces of water on an empty stomach at least one hour before, or a minimum of two hours after meals. Follow it with another eight-ounce glass of water, because like flax and chia seeds, they absorb a ton of water.

Any kind of fiber will decrease your appetite and clean you out. When taken with enough water, it speeds up transit time (how quickly food gets eliminated). You'll feel fantastic! Fiber, protein, and greens are not only key to health, but also to successfully maintaining your weight long-term. Fiber fills you up and satisfies you. Remember to increase fiber slowly, including fruits and vegetables, to avoid digestive discomfort. Don't let a little gas put you off. The health benefits are well worth the short-term adjustment. If you increase slowly, you should be fine. Digestive enzymes usually decrease gas and bloating.

Mindful Piggy Playtime

Smoothie Recipes

Now that you understand the main components to make delicious, healthy smoothies, here are a few recipes to give you an idea of how you can put them together.

Tarika's Go-To Smoothie

- 1 scoop of your favorite protein powder (rice, whey, raw protein, etc.)
- 1 serving fruit (berries, apples, pears, bananas, mangos, pineapple, etc.)
- 1-2 Tb. flax or chia seeds (soaked or ground)
- 2-3 Handfuls of greens (use whatever you fancy)
- A dash of cinnamon, or your favorite spice
- A pinch of salt (optional)

Add water, unsweetened nut or grain milks, low glycemic juices, or a beverage of your choice to desired consistency. Flax and chia seeds thicken over time, so add more liquid if you're not going to drink it right away.

Dairy Based Smoothie (if you're not sensitive, or intolerant)

- ½ cup (or serving) goat kefir, yogurt, ricotta, or cottage cheese
- ½ banana
- ½ cup frozen pineapple, raspberries, or strawberries (or whatever you like)
- 2-3 handfuls of salad or leafy greens
- water or a beverage of your choice (to desired consistency)
- 1 tsp. vanilla extract, rose water, or any other extract or spice

Nut Based Smoothie (if you're not sensitive, or intolerant)

- ¼ cup soaked almonds or 1 Tbsp. nut butter (any nut or seed)
- 1Tb unsweetened cocoa or carob powder (for extra boost)
- ½ banana (fresh or frozen)
- 1 cup frozen berries (berry/cherry blend from Trader Joe's is my favorite)
- 2-3 stalks raw kale, or any salad or leafy greens
- 1 scoop green powder supplement (optional)
- 1-2 Tb. flax or chia seeds (soaked or ground)
- 1 tsp. vanilla extract

If you include some type of protein, fruit, fiber, and greens you can't go wrong. Play with it and enjoy nourishing yourself! You can vary your ingredients, depending on what's in the fridge, your mood, and appetite. Once you get the hang of it, you'll be elated with your satisfying creations.

Smoothie Ingredient Options

To make it even easier for you to come up with your own recipes here's a list of basic ingredients. Choose at least one ingredient from each category until you find killer combinations.

Proteins	Fruit and Vegetables	Fiber and Nuts	Liquids	Spices and Superfoods
Protein powders: whey, Rice, Pea, or sprouted grains.	Any kind of fruit: fresh or frozen. Small amounts of dried fruit.	Psyllium, Chia seeds or Flax seeds.	Unsweetened nut or grain milks	Cinnamon, Cardamom, Mesquite powder, Maca root, carob, or cocoa.
Dairy: Cottage Cheese, ricotta, Yogurt, Kefir, or Milk if tolerated.	Trace amounts of natural sweeteners like Maple Syrup or Honey.	Any kind of nuts or seeds, or nut/seed butters.	Coconut Water, Milk	Rose Water, Vanilla, or nut extracts.
Eggs, Egg whites	Avocado, Zucchini, anything green.	Dried Coconut	Water, unsweetened fruit juice (in small amounts mixed with lots of Water)	Green food supplements, probiotics, Bee Pollen.

Scrumptious Salad Bar In Your Own Fridge!

If you're not into smoothies this might be the perfect cooking activity for you! This has become a pillar that guarantees many of my clients, and myself ample nutrition, greens, and fiber.

I always have a variety of fresh ingredients and premade salads in my fridge. I use my Cuisinart to shred cabbage for coleslaw, grate carrots, and grind parsley or basil to make homemade pesto. I make a few things at a time to save time cleaning equipment. Sometimes I make Mexican-style chopped salad with zucchini, fresh corn, red peppers, and cilantro. I make salad dressings from a variety of vinegars, oils, nuts, seeds, avocado, zucchini, fresh herbs, and spices. I keep them separately, so that my salads stay fresh and crisp for days.

Once you get into a rhythm of grating, slicing and dicing vegetables, I think you'll find your efforts worth the scrumptious salads you can create within minutes, at any given time.

You can experiment by making hummus, nut pastes, and bean dips to add creamy textures, and to avoid getting board of plain salad. You can pre-cook a variety of legumes, like garbanzo beans, lentils, and black beans for when you want to turn it into a meal.

I've sprouted legumes, nuts, and seeds for nutritious variety and texture. I've toasted pumpkin, sunflower, and sesame seeds in tamari to add delicious, nutty textures. When I want to turn a salad into a trail mix treat, I add dried or fresh fruit. I soak seaweed and steam veggies to make exotic Asian salads. I prewash my greens, dry

160

them in a salad spinner, and store them in airtight glass containers. I can satisfy my hunger after long, strenuous days as soon as I get home!

You may also like to have grated cheese, feta, avocado, olives, and artichoke hearts on hand. Palm hearts, pickles, sauerkraut, boiled eggs, or cooked meats are great too. Beets, boiled potatoes, or other steamed vegetables make fantastic additions.

When I don't have time to make dressings I use olive oil and lemon or vinegar. Occasionally I buy a healthy premade dressing for variety. When I have a little extra time at the grocery store I look for new dressings, healthy sauces, and spice mixes to make things exciting and flavorful. The right blend of flavors can turn any basic ingredient into a mouthwatering masterpiece.

I recommend reading labels and avoiding refined Sugars and trans fats. Trans fats are hydrogenated vegetable oils that lower good cholesterol (HDL) and raise bad cholesterol (LDL), putting you at higher risk for heart disease. Hydrogenation turns what would normally be a healthy fat into a manmade substance that sticks to your arties, damages cells, and is difficult to metabolize and eliminate. In some countries they're illegal. Trans fats are mostly found in baked goods, premade sauces, dressings, candy, and snack foods. They're often listed as partially hydrogenated oil.

You may also want to look at the caloric value of a food to make sure it's not full of fat or high in carbohydrates. I recommend buying organic whenever possible, and making sure everything listed is natural (a recognizable food found in nature). If you're not familiar with an ingredient and you can't pronounce it, it's probably manmade. Artificial ingredients are generally difficult to digest, addictive, increase your appetite, make you hold water, gain weight, and they can be carcinogenic.

Mindful Piggy Playtime: Make Two Meals At a Time

Here's another Mindful Piggy Playtime that can ensure easy nourishment. Simply make enough for two or three meals at a time. You can make extra vegetables; precook whole grains, or barbeque meats. Then you can vary your uses of leftovers to make each meal unique.

Mindful Piggy Playtime: Hearty Soups and Stews

If you don't mind eating the same thing for a few days, or you cook for a family, you can make a weekly pot of soup or stew. You can also freeze portions of it, or take breaks, as most stews, depending on the protein you add, stay fresh for several days. You can use endless combinations of vegetables, proteins, herbs and spices to make extraordinary concoctions.

I love legumes. I eat a large variety of beans and lentils as they're incredibly satiating, particularly in cooler climates. If you're into legumes, try and soak them overnight, or longer if you like. Once I soaked black beans for almost two days, and they were fantastic. Rinse them well before cooking because some beans, black beans in particular, have toxic substances and enzyme inhibitors that get released while soaking. Soaking legumes makes them easier to digest, faster to cook, and gives soups a smooth, creamy texture.

I especially love to cook them with finely chopped onion and Kombu, Japanese seaweed that tenderizes them, adding a creamy, rich texture. I use vegetable soup stock as a base, and blend delicious combinations of organic vegetables. In summer I generally keep legumes plain to add to salads, or for hummus and bean dips.

Mindful Piggy Playtime: You Never Know When You, or Your Family Will Get Hungry

Having a variety of healthy snacks available like nuts, washed fruit, crackers, dips, cheese, eggs, or whatever else you like to eat, is another excellent strategy.

If you have children, blood Sugar irregularities, and only eat when you're hungry, you probably know how important this is.

I often carry food with me, because my hunger varies from day to day. Sometimes I can hardly finish the healthy lunches I bring to work, and other times I need twice as much food. I take a small, insulated cooler (looks like a camera bag) with an ice pack to work every day. My food stays cold and fresh for hours, even in hot weather, so nothing goes to waste.

Taking more than you need enables you to let go of the fear of scarcity and break habits of overeating.

Cooking with Love Summary

Transform cooking from a chore into a joyful, creative activity. Find ways to make it fun and interesting, so that you look forward to it. When you cook connect with your heart, letting love flow from your hands, so that it infuses your food with love.

Connect with creativity to plan and prepare your favorite foods and recipes, so that you have healthy nourishment at every meal. Connect with your body intuition and creativity, so that you find healthy ways to satisfy your needs, and others you may be cooking for, without compromising too much on flavor and textures. Focus on one cooking strategy at a time until it becomes routine, and then another to build a healthy foundation.

Nutrition Tip: 2. Get Sugar Savvy

The average American consumes 22 tsp. of added sugar a day, amounting to an extra 350 calories! Look out for added sugars in packaged foods. Sugar-sweetened beverages and breakfast cereals are the worst offenders. Most people don't realize how much added sugar they contain.

However, even though cutting back on added sugars is vital, the body doesn't distinguish between natural or added sugars, so paying attention to total sugar is key. You can get too much sugar from fresh or dried fruit, or honey and maple syrup for example.

Harvard T.H. Chan School of Public Health

http://www.hsph.harvard.edu/nutritionsource/carboh ydrates/added-sugar-in-the-diet/

Chapter Seven

Divine Eating; A Mindful Eating Experience

Why is food so deeply associated with love? Do I need to separate them to have a healthy, enjoyable relationship with food? Is it what you eat, or the state you're in while eating that triggers compulsion versus satisfaction? Does nourishment come from food, or can it come from many sources?

Linda's Success Story
Being reminded to breathe before eating brings the act of creating a meal into a mindful, relaxing chewing experience. Looking at my wonderful creation, thinking how I grew some of the food on my plate and am responsible for the inspiration I am putting in my mouth, has brought me to pure excitement for the food I eat. Gratefulness is the feeling I receive in this moment.

Linda Mazur

This chapter helps you become mindful while eating, which is the most important moment of all! Even if you make excellent choices at the grocery store and cook most of your meals, if you eat more than your body needs, or fall victim to unhealthy cravings, you'll suffer the consequences.

These meditations help you connect with your body while you eat. Eating mindfully is all you need to transform your body. And you can become mindful in any moment.

Eating gives you a precious opportunity to commune with your body, food, and God. Food is full of nature's miraculous forces– rain, sun, nutrients from the earth, and wind. You can deeply absorb and become one with these divine elements with each healthy, or unhealthy bite. God isn't only available to you when you're being "good". These meditations teach you how to connect with deity even when you're binging on Chocolate!

I first identified Piggy and Watchdog while I was eating. Piggy's frantic energy became obvious when I recognized the speed and compulsion that drove me to gobble down enormous quantities within minutes, before I even realized whether I was hungry. Even though Watchdog was driven by fear instead of greed, and denied me the pleasure of eating, it led to the same consequence: being disconnected from my body. Slowing down and savoring my food enabled me to feel satisfied with wholesome foods in reasonable quantities, which is the purpose of these meditations.

Meditating while you eat expands your awareness, giving you insights about your body and eating habits, while revealing vital keys for you to transform them. The easiest time to connect with your body intuition is while you eat. You can literally feel your body communicating its needs. Food can smell or look enticing, or unappealing, depending on what you need. You receive the signal of fullness when you eat, which is a far more effective and enjoyable way to maintain your weight, than dieting or committing to pre-determined amounts of limited foods. Your nutritional needs vary, depending on numerous factors, so I believe, that freedom and fulfillment come from following your body's wisdom.

When you're overeating and you connect with your body with sensitivity and care, it doesn't feel good to eat more than you need. It's much more satisfying to follow your body's instincts.

Your body will tell you when it's had enough, if you pay attention. It's important to identify the ways in which your body communicates with you. You may get a feeling of fullness in your belly, even though your mouth may still be watering, particularly when you eat addictive foods. Or you may get a sense that it's time to stop eating. In time you'll become familiar with your body's signals, and it will become easier and easier to follow them.

You'll probably notice that when you're overeating you're not really enjoying it, because hunger, like love, is an ingredient you can't outshine.

Have you noticed how much better food tastes when you're hungry? And how even the finest gourmet cooking isn't that appealing unless you're hungry?

The Divine Eating Experience enables you to connect with your body, so that you can select the right foods, and stop when your body's had enough, regardless of where you are, whom you're with, or the alluring delicacies that beckon you.

Signals of Hunger and Fullness

Normally we think we need to eat less in order to lose weight. That's often true, but if your strategies aren't working for you perhaps it's time to forget about dieting, and learn to trust your body's signals of hunger and fullness.

168

Dieting typically makes us gain weight in the long run. Caloric restriction slows down metabolism, and we usually begin to crave all the "forbidden" foods on our diet. Dieting is Watchdog's foremost strategy for weight control. Watchdog is trying to help us, but if we don't find healthy ways to satisfy our needs Piggy will just keep eating, because that's all it knows.

It may take a while for you to trust your body, but I promise it's well worth it! Your body's wisdom enables you to maintain your weight naturally, without feeling deprived.

Have you ever ignored your hunger and eventually caved into your cravings because you couldn't stand feeling hungry any longer? Take a moment to remember a time in the past when you ignored your hunger. Was it an effective, enjoyable strategy? You probably lost weight initially, but was it sustainable?

There's nothing wrong with Watchdog's strategies, it's just important to recognize whether they're effective. Are you getting the results you want?

I spent years dieting and bingeing; until I realized that following my body's wisdom, in combination with a satisfying rhythm of eating, was the only way I could maintain a comfortable weight. I'm assuming you're seeking a new solution, and that you've begun to recognize that your strategies don't work, or at least there's room for improvement.

It's important to give yourself permission to eat. When we feel fat we often feel ashamed because we think we don't deserve to eat. Watchdog deprives us of food in an attempt to stop Piggy from overeating. When we're worried about getting fat we can't enjoy what we're eating. When we don't receive nourishment from food, we don't feel satisfied, hence we want more. So, Watchdog actually makes Piggy eat even more!

Who the heck wants to be hungry all the time? Sooner or later you seek relief from Watchdog's control by giving into your cravings, don't you? Even though food is designed to fuel our bodies, a healthy relationship with food includes eating for pleasure. The problem is that we're out of balance, and we've associated "treats" with rich foods, like cake and ice cream because they're more stimulating than vegetables, but if you give it time your taste buds will readjust to nature. You'll feel so much more satisfied eating foods that make you feel good.

What Makes Eating Pleasurable?

Wholesome foods become more pleasurable than additive indulgences when you pay attention to your body, and value how different foods affect you. Think of a meal you thoroughly enjoyed recently that made you feel great. Did you eat junk food, or was it a delicious, balanced meal?

Feeling good and eating healthily is an intrinsic need. Feeling energized and satisfied is much more fulfilling, than eating refined foods that leave you depleted and craving more, isn't it? When you eat junk food, the part of you that wants to live fully and be your best, suffers, doesn't it? We want to feel good after we're done eating.

You can experience tremendous pleasure from eating simple foods, like tomatoes, when you're connected to your body. The next time you eat comfort foods, pay attention to see how much they soothe and relax you. Then notice how you feel when you eat what your body needs. As you become more mindful, it gets easier and easier to choose foods that make you feel good.

Many of us have a habit of relying on food for emotional nourishment, which is another way we seek pleasure from eating, but food can't satisfy us emotionally. Our deeper needs, which trigger emotional hunger, can only be satisfied with things that are emotionally nourishing, like love, our inner being, fulfilling connections, and for some, cuddling with a pet. Food is inherently emotionally satisfying to a certain degree, which is why it's easy to confuse it with physical nourishment, but here again, balance is key. Once you discover which foods are the most satiating physically and satisfying emotionally, you can dance beautifully within realms of healthy, pleasurable eating. Choose wisely, and primarily eat when you're hungry and stop when your body has had enough, so that you can enjoy your festive favorites without gaining weight.

You don't need to follow Watchdog's rules and make perfect choices all the time to get results. Just don't let pleasuring your taste buds become a habit. Focus on making choices that make you feel good and enjoy concentrated foods as a luxury, when you really want them.

I think the biggest cause of weight gain is emotional eating– eating for reasons other than physical hunger. When I'm in Italy I adapt to their food culture and to what's available. One year I ate things that I hadn't allowed myself to eat in California, like vegetables drenched in oil, cheese, pizza, wine, and Chocolate. I balanced the rich foods with salad and steamed veggies, and ate smaller portions. I actually lost weight, drinking wine every night, and eating cheese and Chocolate!

I realized that in California I'd end up eating all those foods, in bigger quantities (a bar of Chocolate versus one Baci), because of the tension and allure that comes from restriction. Watchdog made me feel ashamed when I ate highly caloric concentrated foods, so I'd disconnect from my body as a way to avoid feeling bad about myself. Being disconnected from our bodies makes us eat much more because we never feel satisfied. We keep eating in an attempt to connect with ourselves.

Ignoring Hunger Makes You Overeat

The problem with ignoring hunger for too long is that our body's survival mechanisms—which are far more powerful than Watchdog's control—eventually, make us overeat. That's what made me eat several desserts a day when I was a dessert chef in Sedona.

Don't wait until you're ravenous; eat when you're comfortably hungry. You're probably thinking that's a paradox. "How can I be comfortable and hungry?" Many of us avoid hunger like the plague. We eat when we're not hungry, and we overeat to avoid hunger. Hunger is a form of tension, so it's understandable we try to avoid it, but when it becomes a habit we gain weight. Having healthy food available enables you to wait until you're hungry, instead of eating because it's time to eat, or because you're afraid to get hungry later. When you have

172

healthy food available, hunger is a joy, a delightful opportunity to nourish yourself.

It's healthy to be a little hungry at times; it gives your body a chance to burn stored energy and your digestive system a break. Just make sure you don't let yourself get too hungry, because that too can trigger overeating. Slight feelings of hunger pass, even if you're not able to eat right away. If you never let yourself get hungry, you're probably eating too much.

What's your relationship to hunger? Do you let yourself get hungry, or do you avoid it by eating frequently, large quantities, or rich foods? If you don't know when your next meal will be, do you have a tendency to eat more? When you have plenty of delicious food available do you eat less because you know you can eat again later? Or does having a lot of food around make you eat more? I've often given myself permission to eat less, while giving myself permission to eat again later if I get hungry. Surprisingly, the less I eat, the less hungry I am. Our bodies are phenomenal at adjusting to the types and quantities of foods we eat! I've also eaten more because of having too much food around. After eating three dinner's worth of veggie-legume stew for breakfast, several times in a row, I identified the types and quantities of foods I needed to prepare to be relaxed and eat less overall, without being tempted to overeat, or eat when I wasn't hungry.

The other reason you need to wait until you're hungry is so that you can stop when your body's had enough. When you eat when you're not hungry, it can take enormous quantities to feel satisfied, because you didn't need food in the first place. Eating when you're not hungry is another way of overriding your body's wisdom.

Being a compulsive eater makes stopping when your body's had enough particularly challenging. Many people eat more than their bodies' need occasionally, but when it becomes a habit there's consequences. Not stopping when your body's had enough is another way we ignore our body's wisdom.

A healthy relationship with food is eating when you're hungry and stopping when your body has had enough. It's simple but not always easy. To make it easier, let's break it down into bite-size steps. It's helpful to start by focusing on waiting until your body's hungry before you eat. Get to know what hunger feels like, how does your body tell you its hungry?

When I'm hungry my mouth waters and I start thinking about food, or picturing what I want to eat. Sometimes I feel hunger as a need, impatience, or restlessness, particularly when my blood Sugar is low. Some people feel lightheaded, dizzy; find it difficult to concentrate, or their belly growls. There are different levels and signs of hunger. Become familiar with yours.

Ideally, you should eat before you feel light headed. If your body goes into starvation mode, you may experience powerful cravings, which can seem impossible to resist. When you wait that long it can take large quantities to feel satisfied, similar to when you eat when you're not hungry. The art is to eat when you're moderately hungry. On a scale of one to five, one being ravishingly hungry and five being full, it's best to eat at level two or three, and stop at four. However, please don't make rules from these suggestions. If Watchdog takes the hunger scale too seriously and you become rigid, Piggy might rebel. The key is to experiment while connecting with your intuitive wisdom, until eating when you're hungry, and stopping when you've had enough becomes second nature.

Remember, your heart is what enables you to receive signals of hunger and fullness. Your heart is the door to Piggy and Watchdog's innate qualities, which make it easy to follow your wisdom, and stop when your body's had enough.

Responding to Hunger

Hunger is a powerful urge designed to keep us alive! Your heart can momentarily delay your response to hunger, so that you can make empowering choices instead of going on automatic. When we react to our impulses in unconscious ways, either Watchdog ignores hunger or Piggy overeats.

You need to connect with your heart, especially in moments of emotional hunger. Emotional hunger can feel like physical hunger, because our emotions affect us physically. Have you ever noticed how anger can increase your heart rate, and how stress can make you grind your teeth?

The differences between emotional and physical hunger are so subtle that it probably wouldn't be helpful for you to identify right now. They both feel like hunger. Your heart will reveal whether your hunger is physical or emotional, and how to respond in each situation. As your awareness grows you'll become attuned to recognize the difference.

If you're physically hungry, you'll feel it. Your body will tell you when it's time to eat, and what it needs. If you're hungry and there isn't any food available, your heart will help you relax until you can eat.

Without the heart we react to hunger as if we're going to starve to death. We assign meaning and blow it out of proportion, instead of just feeling it as a physical sensation. Piggy gets afraid of feeling deprived because of all the times Watchdog prevented us from eating when we were actually hungry. The tension and urgency of hunger can make you grab foods that aren't right for you, and overeat.

Emotional hunger is Piggy begging for attention. In your heart you can embrace Piggy, so that you feel cared for and loved. You become less focused on food, and sometimes you realize you weren't even hungry.

Normally Watchdog tries to control and dominate Piggy, and you loose touch with your body's wisdom. That's one of the reasons we get confused and mistake emotional for physical hunger. Piggy and Watchdog can't determine whether you're hungry, or what your body needs. You need to bring love and care to the impulse, so that you don't get caught in judging yourself, evaluating whether you deserve to eat, or fearing negative consequences based on your past reactions to hunger. Your heart gives space to the impulse, so you can connect with yourself, without being taken over by old habits.

Becoming aware of the nature of hunger helps you relax and make smart choices. Loving awareness connects you to something bigger, beyond the little fragment of your personality wanting something. When you're emotionally hungry connect with your heart, so that your emotions can pass, or be transformed. Hunger comes and goes. When there's less pressure to eat, you'll be able to feel your emotional needs, and find more fulfilling ways to satisfy them.

Responding to Hunger Meditation

This meditation connects you to your heart, so that you can discover whether your hunger is physical, and respond to your needs intelligently. When your hunger is emotional, your heart enables you to feel the sensations of emotional hunger and let them pass, as you are nourished by something greater and deeper.

The next time you're hungry take a few moments to connect with your heart. Take long, slow breaths, feeling the physical sensations of hunger and the impulse to eat.

> ❖ Place your hand on your heart. Your soothing touch lets Piggy know that it's cared for and loved.
> ❖ Let your heart expand to embrace whatever you're feeling. Allowing the sensations of hunger to be surrounded by the loving tenderness of your heart. Resting here, giving time and space to your impulses, as the feeling of hunger and the impulse to eat are permeated with love.
> ❖ As you relax, you are opening to your inner strengths, giving you the sensitivity to feel, and choose what's right for you. Let your body tell you what it needs. If

177

your hunger is emotional, continue to
connect with loving care. Notice how
nourishing it is to connect with the love
inside your heart.

Mindful Watchdog Activity: Eating When You're Hungry

Connect with Watchdog's essential nature and
Piggy's feeling nature. Piggy gives you the sensitivity to
feel your body. It's Piggy's nature to feel. Piggy feels
sensations of hunger, as well as feelings of pleasure,
love, and joy.

Watchdog can't feel. Watchdog can easily go a
whole day without food before it realizes you're
ravenous. However, you need Watchdog to break habits
of emotional eating. Watchdog's essence gives you the
strength and determination to wait until you're hungry.

Piggy would eat all the time, if you let it. Piggy eats
when it feels like it, whether your body is hungry or not.
Piggy likes to feel full. The next time you're hungry, be
aware of the push-pull between Watchdog and Piggy,
and pay attention to what your body needs. How does
your body "tell" you when it's time to eat? Does your
mouth water, or do you feel it in your belly? Do you start
thinking about food, or picturing what you want to eat?
Pay attention to how food tastes and your enjoyment of it
when you wait until you're hungry. Is it easier to stop
eating, and do you feel more satisfied when you wait
until you're hungry? When you fall back into habits of
overeating, notice what that feels like.

You may find times you resist eating when you're
hungry and moments you eat emotionally, or out of
habit. Please don't judge yourself. Take the opportunity

to bring loving awareness to your old habit by connecting to your heart.

The next time you eat, wait until you're hungry if you can. If you've overeaten it may take longer, but don't worry, your hunger will return and food will taste great again! You may want to take notes about your observations and insights. Writing is a great way to become more mindful. You can also share your new understanding with a friend. I learn a lot from talking to others.

Receiving Signals of Fullness

Once you can wait until you're hungry at least some of the time, become attentive to your signals of fullness. Get to know how your body "tells" you it's had enough. The Divine Eating Experience meditation, near the end of this chapter, will guide you through this.

Signals of fullness can be different for everyone in the same way hunger varies. The signal of fullness can feel like a gentle nudge, or you may get a sense that it's time to stop eating. The voice of your intuition may softly whisper, "It's time to stop." You may see your signal of fullness as a symbol, like a smiling Buddha with a hand on its belly, or you might see yourself pushing your plate aside. Perhaps you feel the sensation of fullness in your belly, or food loses its appeal and doesn't taste as good, like when you eat when you're not hungry. The body has incredible wisdom; even your taste buds reflect appetite and satiety.

You may receive the signal of fullness differently each time you eat. My signals vary, but the more balanced I am, the clearer they become. Even after you

179

receive the signal of fullness you may still feel waves of desire. Piggy's desire for more usually screams louder than the signal of fullness, at least initially. As you learn to trust your body and follow its wisdom, instead of Piggy's cravings, your body intuition will become clear. Soon it will feel better to respect your body than to stuff yourself with food.

It can take twenty minutes, or longer for your brain to receive the signal of fullness from the nerves in your stomach. That's why it can be challenging to stop eating. The good news is it gets easier. The less you overeat, the stronger your signals become. Stopping when your body's had enough can be challenging for all of us. I created these meditations when I realized I was compulsively eating large quantities at every meal! I didn't know how to stop after a reasonable amount.

I ate healthy food and exercised intensely every day, so that I wouldn't gain too much weight, but I wasn't happy. I wanted freedom. I needed to learn to feel my emotions without numbing them with food, which is what we'll be doing in chapter nine, Satisfying Cravings in Healthy, Fulfilling Ways. I wanted to be able to choose what, when, and how much to eat based on my body's needs, rather than eating to try and fulfill my unmet needs. I wanted to feel confident and beautiful regardless of whether men were attracted to me, instead of starving myself in order to feel loved, or stuffing myself to drown out feelings of loneliness. After a while it wasn't even about being skinny, it was about being healthy and at peace.

I realized I didn't know what it felt like to be comfortably satisfied without under, or overeating. I spent so many years ignoring my body's signals that I lost touch with its wisdom. I ignored multiple signs of hunger and fullness, and then ate until I was stuffed. I wasn't connected to my body when I ate because of my painful history with food. You can see how confusing it must have been for my body. When you're disconnected from your body, it's very difficult to receive and respect your signals of fullness. You receive your body's wisdom when you're connected to it.

These meditations help you become present to your body as you eat, so that you receive your wisdom and feel satisfied. We think our problem is that we enjoy food too much, which is partly true, but when we overeat, it's usually because we're not savoring our food, or we've waited too long to eat, or haven't waited long enough. Waiting until you're comfortably hungry and taking time to enjoy your food is what's truly satisfying. But don't take my word for it. Find out whether this is true for you too.

Prayer of Grace

I created Prayer of Grace, a 2-minute meditation to give you quick and easy way to connect with your body before you begin eating.

Prayer of Grace is a beautiful, elegant way to begin your meal. It pauses the stresses of your life, giving you time to connect with yourself, so that when you eat you're nourishing your body and soul.

Prayer of Grace is about coming into the moment and connecting with your heart, so that you can receive your body's wisdom. Prayer of Grace connects you with gratefulness, which is a simple way to connect with your heart. You can always find something to be grateful for, even when you're feeling hopeless and caught in negative mindsets. Gratefulness is like drawing the curtains and letting sunlight into a dark, gloomy room. You instantly feel better. Even if you can only let a little light in, that can be enough to connect with yourself.

After saying your prayer a few times, pausing and appreciating your meal before you eat begins to happen naturally. When I begin my meals with a Prayer of Grace I rarely overeat because my body tells me when it's had enough.

Make nourishing your body a priority and you'll be richly rewarded. Be generous with yourself– take time to shop, plan, and prepare your meals. Make time for meals, so that you feel satisfied, especially if you're eating less in order to lose weight. Don't miss an opportunity to nourish yourself! Treasure and look forward to each eating experience as if it's your first meal!

I schedule meals. I don't distract myself with emails, phone calls, or loud music, and I try not to get lost in engaging conversations. I love to share meals and connect with others while I eat, but I tune into my body as much as possible. When I'm not present, I often look down at my empty plate and wonder why I don't feel satisfied.

It's so important to spend quality time eating. Time is so relative. Even when you don't have much time, you can make seconds feel like minutes when you slow down. Have you ever noticed that? And sometimes the opposite is true: minutes can seem like hours. These meditations take you into the timelessness of the heart, so that you can enjoy each moment fully.

When you say your Prayer, take a moment to look at the colors, shapes, and how the food is arranged on your plate. Appreciate the uniqueness of each food, like a beautiful bouquet of flowers. You may like to hold your plate up to your nose, or lean forward to smell it before you begin eating. Make each meal a special, sensory experience.

You can also say a Prayer when you have company. It's a lovely way to set the tone for a social evening with family or friends, especially since saying a prayer is widely acknowledged and appreciated.

Prayer of Grace Meditation

Do this meditation before you begin eating. I recommend following these instructions a few times until you find your own way to center yourself before each meal.

- ❖ Take a deep breath. As you let the air out imagine you're letting go of all your worries and concerns, setting the stresses of your day aside. This is your time, a time for sacred nourishment.
- ❖ As you feel your heart connect with the quality of gratefulness. Perhaps there's something in your life you feel grateful for. As you think of something meaningful, notice how your heart opens.
- ❖ As you feel your heart, look at the food on your plate. Let your eyes be soft and

receptive, like windows, seeing into your deeper nature. Notice whether certain foods look more appetizing than others, as that's one of the ways your body tells you what it needs.

❖ Take another deep breath, opening even deeper, so that you can receive nourishment from the food you're about to eat.

Say a Prayer of Grace before each meal, once a day, or whatever feels right to you. It only takes a couple minutes. Notice whether there's a difference in how you eat. Do you enjoy food more when you take time to connect with your body? You may like to write about your observations to become more mindful of your results.

Divine Eating Experience

I created this meditation after completing a raw food, juice cleanse. During the juicing phase I was only allowed one glass of green vegetable juice per meal, for three days. I obviously wasn't "eating" much, so I experimented with savoring my juice, to see if I felt more satisfied. I sipped it slowly, swirling each mouthful– receiving every drop of nourishment. It opened a door of sensory pleasure and my celery-cucumber juice became heavenly!

Divine Eating Experience gives you an experience of grace, in which you enjoy your food, while feeling nourished and satisfied. I initially designed it to go with Prayer of Grace, but then separated them to give you options. Divine Eating Experience enhances the sensory pleasure of eating, and connects you to your body's wisdom while you eat. It teaches you how to eat mindfully.

Prayer of Grace gives you time and space to let go of your stresses and concerns, so that they don't rob you of an enjoyable meal. They both bring you into the moment, giving you profound sensitivity, and a heightened sense of taste and smell. Are you starting to recognize that meditation is all about being in the moment? When you're in the moment you experience pleasure and joy. When you savor each bite you feel satisfied. Your senses open and you become attuned to your body. You intuitively know what your body needs, moment to moment. When you're connected to your body, you receive your signal of fullness and can stop eating when your body's had enough.

I experienced the signal of fullness for the first time during this meditation. It was a clear message from my body, very different from Piggy and Watchdog's distorted opinions and desires. My body was telling me it was satisfied. A door opened during my cleanse, but after I created this meditation, I realized I had found a vital key of transformation. The Divine Eating Experience broke my lifelong habit of compulsive eating! That's how powerful this meditation is!

You can practice the Divine Eating Experience every time you eat, especially when you're overeating. It may not always stop you in your tracks, but it will help you connect with your body, so that you feel satisfied more quickly. This meditation takes you deeper into your heart, into your source of love, which is often what we're wanting from food. It transforms everyday eating experiences into opportunities to connect with yourself and nourish your body.

Divine Eating Experience Instructions

Do this meditation while you eat. Schedule time for meals, and give yourself at least twenty to thirty minutes without distractions. If you like, you can enhance your eating experience by lighting candles or using your favorite dishes. You may want to buy flowers or pretty tablecloths and napkins. You're special; you deserve to take care of yourself!

If you're not at home, find a quiet corner at work where you'll be undisturbed. This meditation dissolves the guilt and shame we can feel around eating, giving you golden opportunities to connect with your body in a new way. Your body intuition enables you to let-go of ideas about what you should, or shouldn't eat, so that eating becomes nourishing, instead of shameful.

Bring special attention to chewing. You may want to chew each bite twenty to thirty times to see if you notice a difference in how you feel. Chewing helps digestion enormously, because digestion starts in the mouth. Saliva contains digestive enzymes, which start to break down the Sugars in food, so that your brain registers the signal of fullness more quickly.

Divine Eating Experience Meditation

- ❖ Bring your full attention to eating, tasting the different flavors and textures as you chew. Savor each bite. Notice whether certain foods taste better than others, as that can be one of the ways your body communicates its needs.
- ❖ Tune-in to your body as you eat, receiving all the ways in which your body intuition communicates with you. Your body may speak to you in gentle whispers, or as an inner voice. Certain foods may seem brighter, or unappealing, based on whether they're right for you.
- ❖ When you're nearing the end of your meal slow down, so that you can receive your body's signal of fullness. You might see yourself pushing your plate aside, perhaps the food doesn't taste as good, or you might get a sense that it's time to stop eating.
- ❖ Once you receive the signal of fullness, push your plate aside. If you don't receive a signal of fullness, ask your heart to reveal whether your body's had enough.

Mindful Watchdog Activity: Namaste Your Plate

This technique is particularly effective when combined with Prayer of Grace, and, or the Divine Eating Experience. It's a simple ritual to end a meal.

When you receive the signal of fullness gently push your plate aside and Namaste your plate to signify completion. Namaste is when you bring your hands together in front of your face in a gesture of acknowledging the "Buddha", within each of us.

Namaste signifies gratitude, which elegantly circles back to your Prayer, completing a sacred time of nourishment. This simple act of completion breaks old habits of eating past fullness. Ending your meals in a beautiful way is as important as beginning your meals consciously. Stopping eating can feel like you're saying goodbye to a loved one. It isn't always easy, even when you know it's time to let go.

You may need to give space to your attachment by feeling your desire for more. You may want to lick your plate in the same way you'd walk beside a train or stand at a security gate waving goodbye, keeping eye contact with your friend for as long as possible. At a certain point you have to walk away, just like you need to say goodbye to food.

Alvina helped me with this. She realized that no matter how many rye crackers she ate, she always wanted more. She realized she'd eventually need to let go, so why not stop sooner than later? She helped me realize that stopping when you've had enough has a lot to do with letting go—letting go of momentary pleasure and shifting your attention to something other than food.

What helps you let go? What helps you stop when you've had enough? Does hunger play a role? Does it depend on what you eat, how fast you eat, or whether you're connected to your body? You may want to write in your journal or call a friend periodically for support.

Sharing your insights and experiences with others helps tremendously. Remember, it's a journey. Be patient and kind with yourself.

Some people are easier to let go of than others, just like some foods are more satiating, which doesn't always correlate with their caloric content or nutritional value! Sometimes the most satisfying foods have the least amount of calories, and we can't stop eating the high caloric foods like nuts, cheese, and Chocolate!

Food Plans vs. Hunger and Fullness

There are numerous, effective approaches to eating healthily and losing weight. Food plans may seem contradictory to following your body's wisdom, but they can be helpful, and necessary at times. Food plans can bring you into balance, so that it's easier for you to receive signals of hunger and fullness. You can think of food plans as the extra wheels on a tricycle when you first learned to ride. As soon as you find balance, you can ride without them. Ideally food plans evolve into a new way of eating, or continue to be a guiding influence.

They can be as flexible or as structured as you need. Some food plans require you to eliminate or limit certain foods, while others require you to weigh and measure, or commit to meal times.

I needed a food plan at times, because I had no idea what to eat. I didn't have healthy role models growing up, and I relied on carbs and sweets, as most kids would if left unsupervised. Swinging between anorexia and compulsive overeating as a young adult made it even harder to determine what my body needed. Piggy and

189

Watchdog were in charge of eating or not eating, regardless of whether I was hungry. They made choices based on my weight and whether I wanted to be more attractive to men. I needed a food plan to learn how to eat properly before I was able to receive my body's wisdom.

I wanted to feel normal and be able to eat what everyone else was eating. I didn't want to deprive myself in front of others and sneak-eat afterwards. I couldn't trust my instincts. I needed the structure of set meal times and measured quantities for a while. I trained myself to eat three meals a day, instead of starving and stuffing myself sporadically. I ate protein, vegetables, and healthy fats, instead of relying on fruit, protein bars, granola, and yogurt.

Following a food plan helped for a while, but at a certain point I was ready to trust my body. I wasn't able to stick to a plan anymore. For a while I kept making adjustments, thinking there was something wrong with the plan. I tried eating a bigger breakfast, increasing protein, eliminating grains, and a number of other strategies that had worked in the past, but Piggy just rebelled. I was seeking balance, and continually adjusting my plan was reinforcing Watchdog's stringency. Even though food plans can be an excellent tool, in order to respond to your ever-changing needs and environment, it's helpful to learn to follow your body's wisdom. Food plans can help you change your behavior, but you still need to address the emotions and unmet needs that trigger you so establish a healthier way of eating long term.

Emotional hunger can take enormous quantities to satisfy. I rarely snack between meals, because snacks, apart from an apple at 5pm (or something equally satisfying and healthy), aren't part of my plan. If I have a craving at 3pm, and I had lunch at 1:30, I usually wait until 5pm to eat again.

Food plans allow you to relax, so that you're not worried about what, and how much to eat. They free up your energy. When I'm nutritionally satisfied, I have little interest in food between meals. I often don't even think about it. I've obsessed over food my entire life. Food plans can be a blessing– a guardian angel of self-care. So many of my clients constantly worry about what, and how much they eat. If you need help coming up with a food plan contact me through my website: www.TarikaLovegarden.com

Food plans can be helpful and necessary at times, because they give you a break from having to decide what, and how much to eat. They can keep you on track when you don't see results right away, or plateau in your weight. Food plans can be a bridge to become attuned to your body. Satisfying your nutritional needs and finding a convenient, enjoyable way of eating, minimizes cravings and overeating. I measured my food for a while to get a sense of reasonable portions. Now I mostly know how much I need, but I still tune into my body every time I eat, because my appetite and nutritional needs vary. If I fall back into old habits and gain weight, I measure my food for a few meals to get back on track. I generally follow a flexible food plan, because it gives me something to fall back on when I lose touch with my body wisdom. It's evolved into a way of living. The combination of following a food plan and connecting with your body wisdom is where the magic begins. It's healing, effective, and freeing.

I generally have a smoothie, or fruit, fiber, and protein for breakfast. I eat lots of veggies, salad, and approximately 4 oz. of lean protein for lunch. My dinners vary, but they generally consist of mostly vegetables, with some whole grain and, or protein, and salad, especially in the summer.

I thrive with rhythm and consistency. Actually, since I started this work, I notice that most people with an admirable relationship with food naturally follow some type of "food plan". They have meal times, and eat similar foods and quantities, with room for occasional treats. Food plans, as I use and recommend them, aren't diets. They simply provide rhythm and consistency for you to come back into balance. Food plans are a bridge to help you connect with your body wisdom. When you over, or under eat repeatedly your senses can become distorted. There may be times when you don't even know whether you're hungry, or how much your body needs. Food plans are excellent in such times.

When I eat three meals a day, at a similar time, whether I'm mildly hungry or comfortably hungry, I eat less overall. I still pay attention to my body and eat less if I'm not as hungry, but I don't skip meals because that leads to overeating. Skipping meals is another form of emotional eating. It's another way we ignore our body's wisdom. Instead of ignoring signals of fullness, we ignore hunger. I'm not suggesting you eat every time you feel mildly hungry. It's natural and necessary to feel hungry at times. It allows your body time to assimilate what you eat, but when ignoring hunger becomes a habit it can create imbalances, and trigger Piggy.

When I used to restrict myself to one meal a day, I consumed at least 500 more calories. I'd end up eating three meals, plus, in one sitting! When you ignore your appetite and then indulge, your body holds onto every calorie, because it doesn't know when you'll eat again. Your signals of hunger and fullness go haywire. When you have set meal times your body can relax because it knows when you'll eat again. You get appropriately hungry for meals without having to battle cravings in between.

The body is phenomenal at adjusting to our habits, but if we're continually changing what we eat, our bodies get confused. Some days you might skip breakfast, other days you eat a croissant, sometimes you don't eat all day, and then you eat a big meal at night, then the next day you snack, and then you fast, etc. These types of habits disrupt our bodies' signals of hunger and fullness, increase our appetite, and send our bodies into starvation mode. Do your eating habits fluctuate, or do you eat regularly? To stop when your body has had enough is incredibly beneficial, and may be necessary to eat at similar times each day. I do best with three meals a day, with herbal teas, sparkling water, or vitamin drinks in between. Some people do better with frequent small meals, and, or snacks.

One reason many people do better with meals instead of snacks is because the types of foods we snack on are generally not as wholesome as protein and vegetables, for instance. They tend to be less satiating and higher in calories. Experiment with the frequency and timing of your meals, while observing how you feel, until you find what works. When you eat three meals a day, do you feel satisfied with less food? Do snacks help you relax and trust that you'll have enough?

Find the little things that make a big difference. My satisfying beverages are key for me in addition to plenty of water. I also enjoy mint lozenges and pure licorice at the end of, or in between meals. The mints contain a tiny bit of Sugar, but not enough to trigger any consequences. Find foods that give you pleasure without significant consequences, while being mindful of how much you need to feel satisfied.

When you follow a food plan, it's important to connect with your reasons for wanting to eat that way. What will your plan give you, including, and beyond the obvious benefits. Will following through give you freedom from limiting mindsets and unhealthy habits? If your plan enables you to lose and maintain your weight without worrying about food, will you feel more at peace? If you feel drawn to a healthy eating program— go for it! Do whatever helps you come into balance.

There's no right or wrong way to heal. The only thing that matters is that you make choices that are right for you. If you practice following your body's wisdom and increase your healthy choices from 50% to 60%, to 70%, and so on, you'll be zooming down the light road to success! Ideally, I think a balanced relationship with food is eating organic, whole, unprocessed foods that are right for your body 85% of the time, and eating whatever you want 15% of the time, so that you can enjoy food without feeling like you're on a diet.

Pace Yourself

When you're establishing a new way of eating, it can be beneficial, and often necessary to pace yourself by making smaller changes you can sustain, especially if you've dieted and binged. If you need dramatic results to motivate you, big changes may be more effective. It's important to honor where you are. Breaking one habit at a time, and building a healthy foundation is more important than losing weight quickly and reverting to unhealthy habits.

It's a delicate balance. If you don't see results, you probably won't value your efforts, and you may lose motivation. But if you don't pace yourself and feel deprived, you'll likely crave your ol' favorites. Experiment to find balance. You'll know when you've found it, because you'll feel relaxed, see results, and your changes will evolve into a new way of being. If I had connected to my heart while following my plan, it would have been very different. My plan could have naturally evolved into a satisfying way of eating, rather than another set of rules enforced by Watchdog.

There's nothing inherently wrong in Watchdog's strategies. I've found several to be beneficial when combined with meditation. Meditation connects you with the essence, and innate qualities of Watchdog, which are part of your inner being. When you resist Piggy, or Watchdog, they become limited fragments of your personality.

These meditations shift your consciousness, so that you can receive the value of food plans without feeling restricted. The magic isn't in what you do. Your internal state is what makes healthy eating enjoyable and fulfilling. Transformation happens from being in a state of love while you eat, shop, cook, and care for yourself. You still need to change what you eat, but when you're centered in your essential qualities, you can follow a food plan, and your body's wisdom without feeling deprived. As you discover what works for you, you'll naturally fall into a healthy rhythm.

Right now it doesn't matter whether you choose to follow a food plan or your signals of hunger and fullness. The only thing that matters is that you heal. I'm here to help you. Even if you don't follow a single suggestion, but feel more compassion for yourself, I'd be thrilled! Compassion is a quality of the heart, and when you're in your heart you're naturally connected to your body wisdom. The ultimate freedom comes from being able to respond to your needs and situations as they arise, without having to follow a fixed plan. Nobody can follow anything perfectly forever! We can't control life, and most of us, depending on our degree of Piggy, need variety.

If you've lost touch with your body's wisdom, having a routine or food plan can help you become attuned. If you've dieted and can't stand structure, then following your hunger cues is best. To determine whether to follow your hunger cues or a food plan, try both to see what works. Easy is right.

Divine Eating Experience Summary

Connect with your heart and body intuition when you're hungry, to determine what you need. In moments of emotional hunger give Piggy the love it's longing for,

196

so that you can make empowering choices. Schedule meals, and minimize distractions, so that you are attuned to your body's needs. Let your body guide your fork.

Begin your meals with a Prayer of Grace, or listen to the Divine Eating Experience while you eat, so that each meal is nourishing and satisfying. Slow down and chew your food, so that you receive the signal of fullness and can stop eating when your body's had enough. Try a food plan or practice following your signals of hunger and fullness to see what works. Remember, easy is right.

Nutrition Tip: 3. Is red wine really good for you?

They've studied the antioxidant resveratrol found in the skin of red grapes for it's potential heart-healthy benefits on mice, but a human would need to drink more than 1,000 liters of red wine every day to get a similar dose of resveratrol!

Why then do the French, and other Mediterranean cultures drink wine, and have lower rates of coronary heart disease? Is it due to their wine consumption, or perhaps due to much smaller portions and caloric consumption overall, and regular, but much smaller servings of wine, and the fact that their food culture is based on less-than-moderation in term of quantities?

If you've ever stayed with a French family you know that "pigging out" or overeating is simply unacceptable culturally. They slowly sip half glasses of wine and eat small pieces of baguette with slivers of Brie, after several small courses of mainly whole, unprocessed foods. I've observed similarities in the Italian food culture as well.

Mayo Clinic
http://www.mayoclinic.org/diseases-conditions/heart-disease/in-depth/red-wine/art-20048281
Wine Folly
http://winefolly.com/update/french-paradox-diet/

Chapter Eight

Eating Healthily in Social Situations

How can you enjoy festivities, feel satisfied with what you eat, and feel great the next day? Does connection come from sharing the same food, or the people I'm spending time with? It's time to dispel the myth that social situations give us license, and are only fun when we indulge and overeat. Mastering the art of choosing the most satisfying menu options in social situations is critical to feel satisfied, and great the next day. Becoming centered enables you to take care of your own needs, while connecting with others so that you can choose foods that are right for you.

Kelli's Success Story

I participated in Tarika's Meditations on the Fridge six-week program. My biggest struggle was eating healthily in social situations. I travel for work, and I'm constantly going out with colleagues and friends, who tend to order lots of food and alcohol. I found it very difficult to say "no," as I get caught up in the fun.

However, I didn't feel good after coming home from these eating/drinking excursions. Tarika's social situations meditation was wonderful. I was able to enjoy going out with my friends, laughing and having fun, without eating and drinking my way to overconsumption. I didn't eat fried foods and had one glass of wine, instead of a bottle. I made healthy choices like lean fish or chicken, instead of a burger or steak. My friends were supportive of my choices.

Now, when I attend these gatherings I remember the experience I had during the meditation. It reminds me to make healthier choices and skip appetizers and dessert. Furthermore, when I travel I find a grocery store and purchase healthy breakfasts and lunches (like yogurt, fresh fruit and salad), so that I can be lenient at dinner without feeling guilty. I often practice the meditations prior to my trips to remind myself that I can still have fun while traveling, or with my friends at restaurants without coming home feeling unhealthy.

Kelli, San Francisco

This chapter helps you take care of your needs in social, family, or business gatherings, without feeling separate. Social situations have the most unpredictable, and external influences out of all the food-choice-opportunities. Depending on the type of gathering, and who's cooking, you have the least control over the foods being prepared. Other situations contain some external cues, like the sight or smell of food, but they're primarily challenging because of internal influences, like cravings, emotions, and the struggle between Piggy and Watchdog.

Regardless of whether it's a family reunion, business engagement, or an impromptu get-together with friends, each situation offers unique opportunities for you to make empowering choices. The demands of your family, and cultural traditions can make it difficult to tune into to your body and make the right choices. Perhaps pressure at work, or the desire to be seen a certain way by your colleagues can influence your food choices. And, of course, when you're at a party and all your friends are drinking, you can easily feel left out if you don't have a drink.

The issue of not knowing what goes into foods at restaurants or not knowing what to expect at private homes, can seem like Russian roulette to Watchdog, especially when you go somewhere new. Social situations tend to be festive, which can easily trigger Piggy. We frequently make exceptions and eat foods, or quantities we wouldn't normally allow ourselves at home, or in everyday situations. We can get caught in common mindsets, like parties and eating out don't "count", which can make us lose touch with, or ignore our body's wisdom, especially when we drink alcohol.

Alcohol helps us enjoy the moment, but not in a conscious way like meditation. It relaxes and desensitizes us to our pain, by releasing pleasurable neurotransmitters and endorphins. It gives license to Piggy, because we tend to ignore or forget about the consequences of our actions, and seek instant gratification.

A healthy relationship with food doesn't require rigid rules. The important thing is for you to have choice. If you're feeling fat and Piggy wants a brownie, but you've decided to have chicken-vegetable stew, don't you want to be able to make that choice? If you're hung over from drinking too much, too many nights in a row, don't you want to be able to choose whether you'd like to drink? If you think about it, I'm sure you'll find times when Piggy takes over in spite of your resolve, doesn't she?

You've probably experienced instances in social situations where you're not sure what you want and you don't know what to order. Piggy's and Watchdog's conflicting desires can be confusing. When you're surrounded by people eating the foods you crave, or you're with stressful company, it can be challenging to choose foods that are right for you.

This chapter addresses these challenges in great depth, giving you the strength and clarity to know, and ask for what you want. In situations where there aren't any healthy choices available, you learn to connect with your intuitive intelligence, so that you can creatively respond and do the best you can. The key is to connect to what's important to YOU. When you take time to consider your options, and tune in to how you want to feel when you're done eating, it becomes easy to ask for what you want. The momentary fear of embarrassment is replaced by a feeling of strength. Caring for yourself becomes more important. It's much more rewarding to make choices that make you feel good afterwards, than to eat foods that leave you bloated or uncomfortable, isn't it?

These meditations help you become centered, giving you the clarity to choose what's right for you, without being influenced by others, or mouth-watering temptations.

Intuition Is More Effective Than Watchdog's Strategies

You probably have several strategies that help you make good choices in social situations, like skipping Bread, appetizers and desserts, enjoying one cocktail, sharing, or only eating half an entre, ordering lean proteins like chicken and fish, and avoiding creamy and fried foods. Those common strategies are generally effective. However, as you know making the right choices isn't always that simple.

I recently had an important lunch meeting with Antonio (my marketing consultant) to discuss this book. I wasn't focused on food, but I was hungry. Since I was at the top of my comfortable weight range and dating a French/Brazilian Karate champion, even though he found me sexy round or skinny, eating healthily was important to me. I glanced at the menu during short pauses in our engaging conversation. Nothing looked good to me. I considered just ordering two salads, as I had a feeling they'd be small, but I needed protein, so I ordered Cod. I kept thinking I should ask the waiter how the fish was prepared, but I was so enveloped in our conversation, I let it slide. There was nothing more important to me than sharing these meditations.

The fish came. It was deep fried, with a small side salad that was drenched in oil. After trying two tiny bites I realized the freshly baked, warm French Bread was the only thing that looked appealing. I ate a piece of Bread with butter, and a little salad. If I had followed my intuition and talked to the waiter, he may have accommodated me with baked fish and a veggie-rich salad with dressing on the side. Instead, I used my strategy of ordering fish, as that's usually a good option. My disappointment reminded me that our intuition is far more powerful than the best of strategies. Your power comes from your intuitive intelligence. These meditations help you make intuitive, empowering choices in unpredictable circumstances, to give you the best chance at finding options to satisfy your needs. I've tailored each one to address different situations, but their function is the same– they connect you to your inner being where it becomes easy to make choices that are in harmony with you.

The good news about our lunch meeting, in terms of healthy eating, was that I didn't let my mistake spiral into a binge. I connected to my body as I ate, and after two nibbles of fish I pushed it aside. Even though fish is an excellent source of protein, the amount of grease and Breading negated its nutritional value and appeal.

After two small pieces of Bread and a little salad, lunch was over, but I was still a little hungry. In the past I would have grabbed snacks and comfort foods on my way home, but instead, I decided to wait until dinner. I enjoyed a big bowl of nourishing soup and a healthy dessert that night. I felt satisfied. I was also happy with how I handled the rest of the day even though I didn't have the best lunch.

Don't worry if you make mistakes, like I did, by not following your intuition or talking to the waiter before you order. The biggest, most common mistake is when we give up and "go all the way". Remember, it's never too late to make a healthy choice! If you're not enjoying something, throw it away, order something else, or eat less and wait until your next meal.

Are you Being Influenced in Healthy, or Unhealthy Ways?

The manager at my spa casually told me how much he liked popcorn with butter. I kid you not, after his comment I binged on two to three large bowls of popcorn with huge clumps of butter every night for three months! I gained at least five pounds. Just one habit can make you gain or lose weight.

Sometimes I've bought foods I saw advertised on TV that I hadn't thought of in years. I adapt to my boyfriend's eating habits every time I'm in a new relationship, and I take on habits from my family and friends when I visit them. When I travel I adapt to culinary customs. When I go to Italy I drink wine every night, whereas in California, I can easily go months without a drop, depending on whom I'm with.

We're all connected, so it's natural to be influenced by others. However, it's important to become centered, so that you can decide whether, and in which situations, you'd like to adapt. As I said, I enjoy wine in Italy. It's not a problem for me, but in the popcorn example, if I had been centered I wouldn't have binged on it and gained weight.

These meditations help you make choices that are right for you, without being influenced by others, or your environment, unless you choose to adapt. I've gone out to eat after doing this meditation and intuitively known what to order based on how I wanted to feel afterwards.

I knew the fish I had ordered at the Cliff House wasn't right for me within seconds. I actually sensed it before I ordered it, but I wasn't paying attention. Remember, your intuition can come as a soft whisper. Meditation quiets your mind, so that you can receive your wisdom. I rarely eat Bread, but in that case it was the best choice for me. Connecting to what's important to you gives you the strength and intelligence to choose what's right for you each moment.

Asking for What You Want

Barbara went to a nice restaurant for lunch while she was working in Hawaii. She knew exactly what she wanted. She asked for a small steak and a tossed salad with half the dressing. Her server told her they didn't serve steak a la carte, so she ordered the steak on the menu with twice the vegetables, instead of a baked potato. Her server said she'd put the salad dressing on the side. Barbara politely, yet firmly, answered, "No I'd like my salad tossed with half the dressing."

Barbara ate exactly what she wanted, which was half a steak and a tossed salad with half the dressing. She didn't compromise, even though her server wasn't very accommodating. She saved half of her meal for lunch the next day.

It helps to be clear about what you want before you go out, so that you don't get tempted or influenced by others and eat things that aren't right for you. Tune in to your body to determine your hunger level. Notice what you're in the mood for. Then take a moment to tune-in to Piggy and Watchdog, and consider what you need to maintain balance. Have you mostly been in Watchdog eating more simply? Does Piggy want space to order whatever it wants? Or do you feel uncomfortable from too much Piggy eating, and need more vegetables, or something light? What types of foods would bring you into balance? Connect with your heart, so that you can receive your intuitive wisdom. Let your body tell you

206

what it needs, while considering the balance of Piggy and Watchdog.

Once you receive an answer, connect with why it's important for you to maintain balance by eating healthy foods that give you pleasure. Thankfully, most restaurants are accommodating, but even when you're dealing with set menus and inflexible service, you can usually find a way to eat healthily, especially when you know what you want.

Eating Healthily in Social Situations is less challenging for me than stopping when I've had enough, because I'm more of a sneak eater. I rarely pig out in front of others unless they're pigging out with me. I also have a well-developed personality and usually feel comfortable asking for what I want, once I'm clear. We all have different strengths and weaknesses. If this is more challenging for you, take me with you in your heart. You can even ask, what would Tarika order? Asking that question can sometimes be a bridge to your own wisdom. Experiment to find creative ways to make healthier choices.

Connecting with the Essence of Watchdog Meditation

Connecting with Watchdog's essential qualities before you go out enables you to enjoy social situations and feel great the next day. Piggy tends to run wild in social situations, especially when there's alcohol, so this can help you maintain balance.

- ❖ Adjust your body, so that you feel comfortable. Feel your body and notice if there's any tension. Imagine your breath is flowing to tight places, softening and releasing tension back into the earth.
- ❖ Remember Barbara's story, and tune-in to the essence of it. What essential quality was she expressing when she asked for what she wanted? Was she clear, determined, strong, persistent, or creative? What impressed you most about how she ate exactly what she wanted without compromise?
- ❖ Now think of a social situation you're likely to go to. Which essential quality will help you ask for what you want, or find foods that satisfy you without significant consequences?
- ❖ Take a deep breath and connect with this quality inside. As you feel it, let it expand and radiate through your whole body. You may see a color or an image that represents your inner strength, or you may hear yourself asking for what you want.

❖ Take a few more moments to rest in your power. This is the essence of Watchdog.

Let's get practical.

Mindful Watchdog Activity: Asking for What You Want

Before you go out, ask yourself, "Which essential quality will help me make healthy, empowering choices?"

Take a moment to consider the balance of Piggy and Watchdog, and how you can make the healthiest choices that give you the most pleasure. Do you want a night of indulgence, or do you want to feel light, or something in between? Perhaps Piggy wants a glass of wine, and Watchdog wants to enjoy fish and vegetables. It can be helpful to set an intention by deciding whether you're going to drink, and how many you'll have. You may want to consider whether you want Bread, appetizers, or desert. You might want to enjoy a little of each, or one in particular. Do you plan to share an entre? If sharing weren't an option perhaps you'd like to save half of your meal, like Barbara did.

You may want to visualize your ideal outcome for the evening. How do you want to feel when you're done eating? Once you have a plan, think about what you need to be successful. If you plan on skipping Bread and appetizers, will you need a bigger lunch, or a snack, so that you don't feel ravenous when you arrive? If you're going to let Piggy enjoy a night of indulgence, perhaps you want to workout, or have a lighter lunch.

When you get there, tune-in to the menu and ask questions before you order. Connect with the essence of Watchdog and ask for what you want. If the waiter can't accommodate you, use your creativity to do the best you

210

can. It may be worth paying extra for a side of vegetables if they aren't willing to make substitutions.

Eating Healthily at Someone's Home

I've given you lots of guidance for eating healthily in restaurants, but how can you make healthy choices when you're invited to someone's home? Each situation is obviously unique, so even though I'm giving you suggestions, your intuitive wisdom will ultimately determine what's best for you.

Suggestions For Eating Healthily At Someone's Home

Call your host before you go, and tell them your food preferences and needs.

If your host isn't able to accommodate you, bring something to share. You can just bring food for yourself, but bringing something to share, even if that's all you eat, tends to make you feel included.

You can eat before you go, but watching others eat can make you feel left out and trigger common mindsets like: "something's wrong with me," or "I don't deserve to eat." You might also end up eating a second meal, even after you planned not to eat again. I've done that numerous times. I think it's best to find a way to share a meal if that's the purpose of the gathering.

I encourage you to practice taking care of your needs, while sharing meals and enjoying the company of others. There's something intrinsically nourishing and intimate about eating with others. Perhaps it comes partly from sharing entire animals amongst tribes in our hunter-gather days.

Connecting, Regardless of What You Eat

Learning to be centered in social situations, while connecting to others, regardless of what you eat, is essential. How many times have you ordered pizza when you would have been happy with a salad, because you wanted to feel connected to a friend, loved one, or even an acquaintance? Have you felt deprived eating salad while watching others eat Lasagna?

We think we need to compromise to eat healthily and feel connected, or we'll feel separate if we eat what our body needs, while everyone else is indulging, but that isn't necessarily true.

You don't need to eat what others eat in order to feel connected. You can eat what you want and feel connected, or you can eat the same thing and feel disconnected. Even though we mainly connect with others in social situations that are centered on food, it isn't the food that gives us a feeling of connection. They're closely linked in our minds because we often experience them simultaneously, but connection comes from connecting to your essential nature, while melting and merging with others, not from eating the same thing.

Centered and Connected Meditation

This meditation enables you to choose what's right for you; while staying connected to the people you're with. It primarily connects you the essence of Piggy, which naturally connects you with the essence of Watchdog. When you're connected to their essential nature you automatically come in touch with both. Practice this to center yourself before you go out.

❖ Take a deep breath and feel your body, as this will naturally bring you into the moment. Picture a gathering you're likely to go to.

❖ Notice what you're feeling. Perhaps you're already picturing what you want to eat, or you may be feeling defeated just by the thought of what you're going to eat. Maybe you've already decided to give Piggy permission to eat what she wants, or perhaps Watchdog has already chosen a healthy dish you've previously ordered. Feel how your heart embraces whatever you're experiencing.

❖ Connect with the nourishment inside your heart, and feel how love naturally flows between you and others. Imagine you're eating with someone.

❖ Take a moment to connect with your body intuition, by feeling your body, and tune in to what you need. In your heart you intuitively know what will bring balance and harmony.

213

❖ As you select foods that are right for you, stay centered in yourself, even as you melt and merge with the people around you.

❖ Enjoy your inner and outer sources of nourishment, respecting yourself and others for their choices, regardless of whether they match your preferences.

❖ Perhaps connecting with yourself and others is more nourishing than food. Notice how your connection to yourself changes your ability to relate with others.

Eating Healthily in Social Situations Summary

When you're not sure what to order, ask the waiter or your host for recommendations to get a better sense of what might be best for you. If nothing appeals to you, try asking for what you want to see if they can accommodate you.

Remember, connection doesn't come from eating the same foods as others; it comes from many sources. You can enjoy healthy foods while everyone else is eating Spaghetti and meatballs and feel connected. Practice taking care of your own needs while connecting with others while you eat. Think about how you want to feel when you're done eating before you go out and plan accordingly, by investigating menus or eating appropriately beforehand.

Take a moment to connect with your body and intuitive wisdom before you order, so that you're likely to make choices that satisfy you. Give yourself the best chance at successfully meeting your needs, while enjoying connecting with others in social eating situations. Have an individual Skype session or download the Eating Healthily in Social Situations meditation, so that Tarika can help you become centered, ask for what you want, and connect with your intuitive wisdom to make the best choice possible in each situation.

Nutrition Tip: 4. Which type of chocolate has the most calories and fat?

Chocolate has been touted for its antioxidant flavonoids, with chocolate containing the most non-fat cocoa solids being the highest. 3 Tbs. of unsweetened cocoa has about 60 calories, 1.5g fat, 0g saturated fat, and 3g fiber. The equivalent of flavonoids in unsweetened baking chocolate is 1 square (1 ounce), the main difference being the addition of cocoa butter, contains: 140 calories, 14g fat, 9g saturated fat, and 4g fiber.

By comparison, a typical 2-ounce serving of semisweet or milk chocolate (with sweetener and other ingredients added) contains: 270 calories, 17g of fat, 10g of saturated fat. Most of the fiber comes from the unprocessed shell of the cocoa bean. As with all foods that have healthful benefits, remember you're consuming calories, so be careful not to negate the benefits of flavonoids by adding pounds to your waistline.

WebMD, Health By Chocolate, By <u>Elaine Magee,</u> <u>MPH, RD,</u> Reviewed by <u>Louise Chang, MD</u> on March 30, 2007.
<u>http://www.webmd.com/diet/health-by-</u> <u>chocolate?page=1</u>

Chapter Nine

Satisfying Cravings in Healthy, Fulfilling Ways

Isn't it amazing how a perfectly healthy food can become a trigger food, depending on whether you've overeaten that food in the past and your emotional association with it? It's a strange virtue of the body that can either work for or against you that your body will crave more of whatever you eat.

Why would our bodies crave more of the foods we're sensitive to, or that create imbalance, leading to even greater imbalances? Why do you think sometimes you can be satisfied with one piece of chocolate, and sometimes you're still wanting more even after you've eaten an entire bar?

Beth's Success Story

My past two dinners consisted of a green salad with a variety of veggies…beans, snap peas, corn, and cucumbers. The other dinner was an egg salad on an English muffin with carrots, snap peas, and olive hummus. These delicious meals cleaned my body of my food experience over the past few weeks…one of salty and sweet foods.

It started with a bowl of oatmeal and cinnamon toast. The oatmeal was with salt and butter. I noticed a trend. Even though I wasn't eating candy, my meals consisted of salty, and a bit of sweet. For example: Mexican food with a bit of fruit. This went on for a few days and came to a head when I caught myself at an afternoon movie having popcorn and candy. That sent my system over the top.

Perhaps it was a combination of my hormones, and a feeling of Piggy hanging out with me.

I had an interesting experience when I took myself for a foot massage. I was getting hungry for lunch and had a bit of a craving. Not any particular craving, just a craving. After the massage my body seemed balanced and my craving disappeared.

May we continue to hear our bodies speak to us.

Thank you,
Beth, Orange County

Every craving is a golden opportunity to make choices that make you feel good and give you what you really care about. You can choose to give into your craving, walk away from unhealthy temptations, or choose a healthy alternative. Cravings can be messages from our bodies seeking nutritional balance, or Piggy communicating our deeper needs that can sometimes lead to life changes.

Once you start eating, the fleeting moments of pleasure can make it difficult to stop. You can easily get caught in the one-more-bite syndrome, which, of course, leads to many more, as we've all experienced. You can become so engrossed; it can feel like you don't have a choice. "I have to have ice cream NOW!" It's important to recognize that you don't need to fulfill every craving—you can choose how to respond to your impulses.

These meditations connect you with your inner being, so that you can make choices that are right for you. Sometimes you may want to let your craving pass, choose a healthy alternative, or enjoy the foods you're craving. As you discover what Piggy is really wanting, which is usually something other than food, you can satisfy your needs in more fulfilling ways.

Your success in how you respond to your cravings will dramatically enhance your ability to stop overeating. One reason it's easier to make healthy choices in the craving phase, before you start eating, is because the foods we crave are usually addictive. The more we give into our cravings the stronger they become.

When we eat something repeatedly, our bodies begin to expect those foods again, and usually at the same time of day. If you eat Chocolate every day at 4pm, you'll likely crave it every afternoon. Becoming mindful in moments of craving enables you to prevent unhealthy habits from forming.

When you fall back into old habits and eat foods that aren't right for you, it's important to be compassionate with yourself, learn from your mistakes, forgive yourself, and move on. Forgiveness enables you to get back on track quickly, without spiraling into torturous cycles of addictive eating. I will guide you through a Forgiveness meditation in the next chapter.

Instead of being influenced by old mindsets like, "Since you started, one more cookie isn't going to make a difference", you recognize that each craving is an opportunity to care for yourself. Don't use your mistakes as an excuse to continue eating. Leave the kitchen, the grocery store, or order coffee instead of dessert, whatever you need to do to shift to more fulfilling, fruitful activities.

These meditations give you the ability to choose whether you want to eat and what you want to eat, instead of feeling victimized and out of control. When your choices arise from your inner being, it's not a question of will power. Your inner strengths are your power. You're free from battling temptations, giving in, or resisting. You're connected to what's important to you; alert to how different foods affect you, and how good it feels to walk away from food when you need to.

Satisfying Cravings in Healthy, Fulfilling Ways is like building a muscle. As you repeatedly choose healthy alternatives, like water instead of soda, or fruit instead of cookies, you become stronger. As you develop this strength, it gets easier, and in time, your cravings disappear, especially when you stop eating the foods that trigger you.

"Should I try another diet? Perhaps I just haven't found the right one."

How many times have you committed to a healthy way of eating, only to find yourself taken over by cravings? We've all experienced that, especially when we're dieting and hungry. Watchdog decides to go on diet because it knows you'll feel better if you lose weight. It's a logical solution, right? But are you recognizing that Piggy is also trying to make you feel better by eating? Does it work? Perhaps momentarily, but how do you feel after you've eaten a big plate of pasta? They're both trying to care for you in their own, yet often ineffective ways.

When we're craving we often feel conflicted. Piggy wants whatever it wants, whenever it wants it, and

Watchdog restricts our choices and pushes us to exercise. Piggy and Watchdog are vital parts of us. We need to connect with their essence to have a balanced, fulfilling life. You won't be happy if you reject Piggy! Have you ever tried to get rid of that part? Has it worked?

Their influence upon us is only negative when we're out of balance. As soon as you connect with their essence they become healing forces of power and love. I've come to adore Piggy by feeling its essence! Piggy's compassion, warmth, and playfulness feed me every day. You need to embrace Piggy to successfully overcome cravings. Piggy will crave as long as you neglect it. Cravings are one of the ways Piggy gets your attention, a way of communicating your deeper needs. Cravings are opportunities to turn your attention inward and connect with yourself more deeply. Cravings are often signals of imbalance from our body and deeper needs. Sometimes cravings are emotional, and sometimes they're our body's way of asking for nutrition, or because our body craves more of whatever we eat.

Cravings can signal a need for change. You may need a change in your career or relationship, to move location, or shift your focus in some way. Meditation enables you to recognize and respond to these important messages, whether they're from your body or deeper needs. Watchdog needs to be integrated in the same way as Piggy. When you connect to Watchdog's nature, it gives you clarity and strength. Watchdog may not use cravings to get your attention, but it too is trying to maintain balance. In essence, Watchdog gives you choice. It considers the consequences of your actions and evaluates whether the momentary pleasure of eating pizza is worth having to squeeze into your jeans.

Without Watchdog we'd probably just eat and gain weight. However, Watchdog without the heart is control and deprivation, which causes Piggy to rebel. How long can you control yourself before Piggy starts indulging?

This conflict is what makes dieting a never-ending, losing battle. Healthy eaters who don't experience this inner conflict around food may feel conflicted in another area of life. They might struggle with another version of Piggy and Watchdog that expresses itself in their work, how they spend money, or in relationship. For overeaters the conflict between Piggy and Watchdog can sometimes switch from food to another substance or compulsion. A classic example is when a food addict becomes a compulsive shopper, or an alcoholic gives up drinking and starts smoking. Don't switch your obsession to another substance. Practice the meditations in this chapter, so that you can satisfy your cravings, or let them pass by connecting to your heart.

What's Triggering Your Cravings?

Cravings are usually a combination of physical, psychological, and emotional impulses. There are many triggers of cravings. I've simplified them by giving you a summary of the common triggers, and then gone into depth with each category. Identifying what triggers your cravings enables you to find ways to respond to them.

Common Triggers of Cravings

Food Sensitivities– We often crave the foods we're sensitive to. Sometimes habitually eating the same foods makes us intolerant to them, to varying degrees. Are you aware of any food sensitivities, and do you crave more of those foods when you eat them?

Overeating a particular Food– Binging on rice cakes and popcorn for months turned them into one of my trigger foods. One bite, or sometimes just the thought of them triggered a craving. Are there foods you've overeaten repeatedly that trigger you now?

Foods From Your Past– Associating certain experiences with a food can cause cravings. Perhaps you went for family outings and ate ice cream every Sunday afternoon, and now you've linked ice cream with love. Do you crave foods you ate as a child, or in the past?

Cultural Traditions– Perhaps you grew up in a culture that drank wine every night and now you feel like you can't enjoy dinner without it. Maybe rice or Bread was your staple, and without it a meal seems incomplete. Which cultural foods did you grow up with that you crave?

Foods That Are Linked to Emotions

If you eat potato chips every time you feel stressed, neurological pathways may have developed linking them, so now whenever you feel stressed you crave chips. Are there foods you crave in certain situations or when you feel certain emotions?

Eating certain foods with others– I've adapted to my loved ones numerous times; their comfort foods became my trigger foods. Sometimes it took months to stop craving those foods even after our relationship ended. Are there foods you eat with certain people, that you crave even when you're not with them?

Nutritional imbalances– Your body craves what it needs to maintain balance. Are there particular foods, or macronutrients you crave? I used to restrict fats and then binge on nuts for example. As soon as I added more fat to my meals I stopped binging. You'll crave the foods you eat (particularly Sugar and refined foods) until you stop eating them. Have you ever noticed that when you stop eating something, after a few days you stop craving it? The sight, smell, or thought of food– Have you ever been content until you walked past a bakery, or salivated just by thinking of a food?

Dehydration– The parts in our brain that signal hunger and thirst are right next to each other! Sometimes you might just need water when you feel a craving. Unmet needs (need for intimacy, sense of purpose, need for change, etc.) Do your cravings become stronger when you're unfulfilled? If you've noticed additional triggers, or have a variation of the ones listed above, jot them down.

Trigger Foods

A Trigger Food is a broad term for foods that cause cravings, or a desire for more. They're usually refined, or processed in some way. There's often a feeling of dependency, or lack of choice. When you feel neutral about a food it's usually not a trigger food. Trigger foods can become neutral, especially when you eliminate them for extended periods. When you crave a whole food, you may be sensitive to it, seeking nutritional balance, or have an emotional association with it.

Common Foods That Trigger Cravings

- Sugar
- Alcohol
- Wheat
- Dairy
- Nuts
- Spicy foods
- Salty snacks
- Fried foods
- Cheese
- Processed foods
- Baked Goods
- Bread
- Ice Cream
- Chips

Most people's trigger foods fit into the common categories above, whether they're from our past, overeating, or food sensitivities. It doesn't matter how your trigger foods originated, it's simply helpful to become aware of them.

The good news is that once you eliminate, or take a break from your trigger foods, it usually only takes a few days for your body to stop craving them. As you come back into balance, you won't crave those foods, at least not physically, until you eat them again. If you give it time, sometimes those foods become neutral, and you can enjoy them in moderation without activating Piggy.

Satisfying Cravings in Healthy, Fulfilling Ways enables you to decide where, when, how much, and what you want to eat. Please be careful if, or when, you invite your trigger foods back into your life. You may always need to consciously choose when, how much, and how often you eat them. If you consume them regularly or eat large quantities, they can quickly become trigger foods again.

You'll Crave The Foods You Eat Until You Stop Eating Them

Over the years I've identified a strange virtue of the body that can either work for, or against you. Your body will crave whatever you eat. We've survived and evolved as a species because of our body's intrinsic ability to adapt to our dietary habits and environmental challenges. The same virtue that gives us biological insurance and resilience makes us crave high caloric foods. The more you eat, the more you want. That's why cravings can spiral into addictive eating so quickly.

Balance plays an important role in cravings. When I've been eating well and maintaining my weight for a while, my body has greater tolerance. If I've been

226

overeating and nutritionally out of balance my cravings can get out of control. It usually takes a few days of eating protein, vegetables, fruit, and high fiber foods, while eliminating my trigger foods, to come back into balance for my cravings to disappear.

It can also make a difference how you eat your trigger foods. If I eat Bread and cheese on an empty stomach, it's difficult to stop. But if I have Bread and cheese with a big salad, or wine and Chocolate with a balanced meal, I'm more likely to feel satisfied with one portion.

Your Body May Be Seeking Nutritional Balance

Unfortunately, since we've lost touch with our bodies, our minds interpret these important messages as a craving for a food we're familiar with. Your body may be asking for protein, and you crave cheese (which may or may not be the best source of protein for you). Sometimes you crave Sugar when you need protein, which is precisely the opposite of what you need. If you eat Sugar when you need protein, you'll create an even deeper imbalance, and crave more.

Cravings, even Sugar cravings, can sometimes be plain old hunger! Cravings can be your body's way of asking for nourishment, particularly when you let yourself get too hungry. Have you noticed that when you're ravenous and you go to a restaurant it's almost impossible to resist the Breadbasket, or that when you go shopping when you're hungry you tend to buy more than you need, and may nibble on things before you get to the register? It's important to pay attention to your cravings to determine whether your body is asking for nourishment, or whether Piggy needs love and attention.

One of my clients, who had religiously followed a macrobiotic diet for years, came to me when she couldn't stop eating fried chicken on her way home from teaching yoga. It wasn't because she didn't have discipline. Her cravings were most likely her body's way of asking for protein and fat. A macrobiotic diet may be perfect for some, and it may have been right for a while, until her needs changed. Remember to pay attention to your body. Cravings can be your body attempting to find balance.

When I had uncontrollable cravings and gained fifty pounds in six months after following a fat-free diet for years, it was probably because my body was starving for fat and protein. When I went on a raw food diet and binged on large bags of nuts and raisins, and gained several pounds in a couple of days; it was partly because my nutritional needs weren't being met.

When you go on a diet and eliminate, or severely cut out any macronutrient, and binge, it's not because you lack willpower. You're not a failure. Your body's survival mechanisms are just stronger than Watchdog's control. That's why it's much more effective to satisfy your nutritional needs, while addressing the reasons you eat, than to starve yourself dieting.

Piggy May Be Rebelling Watchdog's Rules

Just because you crave something doesn't necessarily mean it's a trigger food. Piggy may just feel like eating ice cream, for example. Sometimes cravings can be Piggy's reaction to Watchdog's control– an attempt to bring you into balance when Watchdog becomes too restrictive.

Have you ever gone on a diet and craved all the foods you weren't allowed? That could be an indication of Piggy going into reaction. Sometimes it's best to allow yourself whatever you want, while paying attention to how different foods affect you. Making choices from understanding takes you into your being, which is beyond Piggy and Watchdog's conflict. Dieting is notorious for triggering subsequent weight gain. It isn't only because caloric restriction slows down metabolism; restriction triggers compulsion.

Emotional Cravings

Emotions are quite possibly the primary cause of cravings. Even though Sugar and refined carbohydrates are addictive, emotional hunger tends to be the root trigger. Unfortunately food can't satisfy us emotionally. Have you ever noticed that when you're happy, you're more likely to feel satisfied with a handful of cherries than a slice of cake, whereas when you're unhappy you can eat all the cherries and cake you want, and you still feel discontent?

If you've relied on food to soothe your discomfort, it can take time to become comfortable with feeling your emotions. The habit of eating to avoid what you're

229

feeling becomes automatic. The impulses of craving become so linked to certain emotions that eating is like a reflex. Emotional eating is the primary reason most diets fail. Unless you connect with your heart to transform your emotions in a natural way, they'll eventually overpower you.

Emotional cravings can seem impossible to resist. They're usually for a specific food. If your craving is emotional and all you want is ice cream, a sandwich isn't going to satisfy you, is it? When you're physically hungry, you might prefer certain foods, but you'd probably be delighted with a sandwich if that's all there is, and depending on how hungry you are. If you pay attention in moments of cravings you'll begin to notice the differences of when your cravings stem from your body, or emotions.

I began to see there was no end to my emotional cravings. When I fulfilled my craving for ice cream, it wasn't long before I craved chips, and soon after that it was Chocolate, or something else, and so on. I realized that emotional cravings couldn't be satisfied with food. When I recognized an emotional craving I made sure to avoid my trigger foods, and tried to wait to eat until I was physically hungry.

This is especially true for those of us who struggle with compulsive eating. Some people are satisfied with one portion of the foods they crave, even in emotional cravings. If that's the case, choose whatever feels right to you. It's still helpful to feel your emotions through your heart, so that they can be transformed instead of numbed with food. If you experience the insatiable cravings I described, I highly recommend avoiding your trigger foods, especially when you're emotional. If you feel you must eat, choose high fiber, water-rich, unprocessed foods as much as possible.

There are two aspects to emotional cravings that are important to address. Our emotions cause cravings, and craving itself is an emotion. Craving is a body sensation that gets loaded with meaning and emotion. You've probably already begun to notice how certain emotions cause specific cravings, like when you feel lonely you might crave Chocolate, or when you feel stressed you might crave Bread. We all have different responses to our emotions, and crave different types of foods. Some people loose their appetite when they feel depressed, whereas others crave their comfort foods in large quantities.

It's important to become aware of your emotional triggers, so that you don't take your cravings too seriously. Once you see that every time you're stressed you want chips, for example, you may want to observe and query your craving. If you were perfectly content before a disturbing incident, your craving is probably just an emotional reaction. As you become aware of your triggers and habits, they become transparent and lose their power over you.

The other aspect to cravings, which is a unique perspective, is that cravings become emotional, especially for someone who struggles with food. The sensation of craving begins in the body. It's a signal from the body– a way of communicating its needs; even hunger can feel like a craving. However, our past struggles with food assign meaning to the sensation of craving and hunger, beginning the battle between Piggy and Watchdog , which is painful. We may feel emotions like hopelessness or fear, because our cravings have led to unhealthy eating and "failure".

A signal of communication from our body becomes an emotional craving. Instead of connecting with our body intuition, our past gets triggered and we get flooded with guilt and shame. We shut off from our inner strengths in an attempt to shut off from pain, which makes us incapable of determining what we need. Your heart gives you space to breathe, so that you can simply feel cravings as sensations of hunger, without activating your past. Your heart can reveal healthy, fulfilling ways to satisfy your body, and emotional needs.

Feeling Emotions Through Your Heart

This meditation guides you deep into your heart, where the emotions that trigger cravings, and the emotions that get triggered by cravings, can lovingly be embraced, while you are centered in something greater. Do this meditation when you feel a craving, or when you feel emotional, so that you can respond to your emotions and cravings with love.

Please don't try and figure out whether your emotions are triggering your cravings, or whether your cravings are triggering your emotions. It's not necessary to make that distinction. Simply feel your emotions, so they can be transformed.

Allowing Cravings To Come, Be There, and Go

Meditation

As you read each instruction, pause for a moment, so that you can deeply receive this transmission of loving awareness. If you like you can close your eyes between each set of instructions.

❖ Place your hands on your heart, and begin by taking deep, gentle breaths into your heart. Feeling each breath creating more space inside, opening to this natural flow of feeling.

❖ Notice what you're feeling. Perhaps you feel delicate movements of energy, or there may be stillness. Allow whatever you're experiencing.

233

❖ Feeling your heart expand with each breath. Feeling your heart's unconditional acceptance of whatever you're experiencing, a vast space that includes the impulses of cravings. Your heart doesn't react, or have an opinion about your emotions and cravings. All is welcome here. Continue breathing, allowing your emotions and sensations of cravings to come, be there, and go, as you are centered in something greater.

Expressing Emotions While Craving

Expressing your emotions is another excellent way to give space to them, so that you can respond to your cravings. Expressing your emotions is particularly important when you feel anger based emotions, or an intense desire. Anger is a very dynamic energy that transforms quickly when expressed. The intensity and heat of our emotions can make it difficult to go in, so expressing them for a couple minutes, before attempting to feel, can be very effective.

Expressing your emotions instead of drowning them out by eating is richly rewarding. Please don't express your emotions with your family and friends, or get into blaming them for what you feel. It's best to do this alone. When you have a craving, take a deep breath and get in touch with what you're feeling. Give a voice to your feelings, and express them! If you're angry with your boss, hit or scream into a pillow. If you're sad go ahead and cry for a few minutes. I cry regularly! If you're afraid of your appetite, shake with fear, and exaggerate it, so that you can see it for what is, and release it. When you feel lethargic, act it out so that your energy begins to flow again.

Emotions can be related to specific events, and sometimes we feel things for no reason at all. Emotions are a natural part of life. There's no need to figure out what's causing your feelings. Simply feel and express your emotions, without assigning meaning. You'll most likely feel relieved after you express them, and they'll pass quickly. You might be angry for two minutes, instead of brooding for hours.

After you express anger sometimes a layer of sadness surfaces. Continue expressing whatever emotions arise until you feel more at peace. At a certain point you will feel better. Keeping your emotions inside, or eating to avoid them, makes them disturbing and obsessive, which often triggers cravings. The key is to connect with your heart as you express them. Your heart is what transforms emotions, and expands your consciousness, bringing you in touch with your strengths. Your heart enables you to feel your emotions fully, without getting overwhelmed by them. When we hold onto grudges, and avoid what we're feeling, emotions fester and come out in unconscious ways, like eating.

Have you ever noticed how quickly a child moves through emotions? One minute they can be smiling, and the next minute they're crying, and then two minutes later they're smiling again! They're not afraid of feeling, like many of us have become. The next time you're craving and you're not physically hungry, pay attention to what you're feeling. What do you really want? Are

235

you eating to avoid feelings, or are you trying to fill a need?

Once you identify why you're eating, pay attention to whether eating is giving you what you want. If you ate a bag of chips because you were board, do you feel more inspired afterwards, or do you still feel board, just fuller? If you ate Chocolate to deal with the pressure of having to meet deadlines, do you feel more productive or are you still stressed, and perhaps, momentarily "buzzed"?

Once you see how unfulfilling unhealthy eating is, healthy choices become more alluring. You may get taken over by old habits at times, but soon you'll look for other ways to meet your needs. The next time you have a craving, stop for a moment and remember what happened the last time you had that craving. Did eating really make you more productive? Or did you get an initial rush, while still feeling burdened by your deadline? How did you feel when your blood Sugar dropped if you ate refined carbs or sweets?

When you see clearly, through your heart, not better or worse, simply seeing yourself and others as they are, you become more intelligent and creative in how you respond to cravings, and life in general. There will be times when you have enough space to allow what you're feeling, and times when your emotions drive you to eat. Don't worry; simply do the best you can. Be as gentle and compassionate with yourself as possible, whether you're overeating or eating healthily. Don't abandon yourself when your cravings take over. That's when Piggy needs your love most! Connect with the loving care of your heart and enjoy eating, so that you feel satisfied more quickly.

I'll be with you in my heart. I deeply understand the pain of overeating, and how difficult it can be to make healthy choices while craving. Love is your greatest power. Love will heal you.

Feeling Fulfilled From Within Meditation

This meditation helps you connect with what Piggy is really wanting in moments of craving, so that you can satisfy your needs in more fulfilling ways.

- ❖ Take a deep breath and place your hands on your heart. Feeling the touch of your hands awakening your sensitivity to feel deeply.
- ❖ Imagine a moment of craving. Notice what you're feeling. Perhaps you're wanting or needing something. Maybe Piggy is begging for treats, while Watchdog is saying no.
- ❖ Take a few gentle, deep breaths, feeling how your heart expands to include both Piggy and Watchdog.
- ❖ Take a moment to find out what Piggy is really wanting, other than food. Do you need love, care, or attention? To discover this, ask yourself, what do I really need right now? Let the answer come to you intuitively.
- ❖ When you receive an answer ask yourself, where can I get this? Will I get it from other people? Will I get it from food? Or can I find it within? Your heart will reveal this to you.
- ❖ Experiment by connecting with your inner sources of nourishment, like love, joy, or whatever you need in that moment. As you feel this quality inside, let it spread

through your whole body, so that it grows. Feel yourself being satisfied from deep within with each full breath you take.

❖ If you still need something from the outside like food, or to connect with someone, you'll be more sensitive and intelligent in how you fulfill that need.

More on The Physical Aspect of Cravings: Sugar

To successfully overcome cravings sometimes it can be vital to understand your relationship to Sugar. Sugar is often the culprit of cravings, addictive eating, weight gain, depression, aggression, PMS, ADD, HADD, water retention, lack of concentration, confusion, lethargy, unstable blood Sugar, low energy, and mood swings, to name to a few.

I'm amazed as I write this list, and there's even more symptoms associated with eating refined Sugar! You may be aware of certain consequences of eating Sugar, and not others. You could be so used to being "under the influence" of Sugar, that you don't even know how good you'd feel without it. Even when you're aware of the negative consequences, are you able to stop? I've never tried heroin, but I wouldn't be surprised if Sugar were as addictive. I consider Sugar a drug, especially for a compulsive eater. I came across an article on a scientific study about rats and cocaine. In the experiment, when given a choice, rats became addicted to Sugar and lost interest in cocaine.

If you're not ready to let go of Sugar, pay attention to how you feel when you eat it. When you see how Sugar affects you, without condemning yourself, you'll likely seek satisfying alternatives. When I eat Sugar it can easily turn into a binge. My last binge of Chocolate-covered Acai berries, that made me gain three pounds, stopped me from wanting Sugar for a while. I simply didn't want to suffer.

You may not be as sensitive to Sugar as I am. If you aren't, then by all means, enjoy an occasional sweet. Find treats that satisfy you and pay attention when it changes, so that you can respond accordingly. For a while, I enjoyed dark Chocolate, and then unsweetened carob chips, protein bars, raw cookies, and then fruit. I've gone for months without Sugar, and then had phases of sharing a dessert once a week, for example. Your taste buds and needs will likely change, continually. It may be helpful to allow yourself a little Sugar, when you really, really want it, in moderate amounts, so that you don't feel deprived. For some, especially for those who feel they "need" Sugar, it may be best to eliminate it completely to break the cycle of dependency, before you can determine whether you can enjoy moderate amounts again.

When I eat Sugar, I'm very careful not to eat it again for a while, so that it doesn't trigger a craving for more, or become an addictive habit. Because I don't eat it often I can get away with eating it occasionally without it triggering me too much. If my cravings become strong, I eliminate it for a while before I enjoy it as an occasional treat again.

When you take a break from Sugar, or other addictive foods, they can lose their appeal. You may find yourself developing a taste for foods you never cared for, because your taste buds regain their sensitivity and appreciation of natural flavors. I never used to like seaweed, kale salad, green juice, and smoothies, and now they're my staples! Not only because they make my body sing with delight, but I actually enjoy them.

Forms of Sugar

Just because something's natural doesn't mean it's healthy. Sugar comes in many forms. In general wholesome forms of Sugar like fresh, or dried fruit are more nutritious than cookies. Highly processed, refined Sugars are stripped of their nutrients and fiber, so they require more energy to metabolize than wholesome forms. Your body has to pull vitamins and minerals from precious stores to metabolize refined Sugar, which depletes you of essential nutrients. In nutrition we refer to candy or refined products as negative nutrition. Refined Sugars spike our blood Sugar, giving us fleeting bursts of energy, followed by depressive crashes that tend to make us tired and lethargic. Then our bodies crave more to raise our blood Sugar, so that we have energy to function.

And of course, need I say it? Refined Sugars are highly addictive. Next time you eat Sugar, versus a piece of fruit, pay attention to your energy level, mood, and cravings. Even though fresh fruit is high in natural Sugar (a bundle of fructose, fiber, Water, vitamins, and minerals), it's usually satisfying. If I'm still hungry I may have another piece of fruit, but I'm not compelled by the I-need-more-now-or-I'll-die craving as with refined Sugar.

Ways to Overcome Sugar Cravings

There are numerous approaches to overcome Sugar cravings. The bottom line is that you'll crave Sugar as long as you eat it. You can either go cold turkey or slowly decrease your intake. If you go cold turkey, I recommend drinking lots of water and taking hot showers, baths, or steams and saunas to minimize withdrawal symptoms. Exercise effectively alleviates symptoms as well. I recommend eating regularly, so that your blood Sugar is stable, and balancing your meals with protein, fat, and fiber. Green vegetable juices can cut cravings instantly. Fresh, or dried fruit, Squash, Sweet Potatoes, or whole grains can be excellent options to satisfy sweet cravings.

Drink plenty of water, herbal teas, and diluted juices (at least 50% water). Breathe deeply when you feel a craving; it will pass. You may want to try taking 500 mg of L-Glutamine, as it's remarkable at cutting Sugar cravings. Chromium can help balance your blood Sugar, but if you eat balanced meals, throughout the day, and you're not diabetic, your blood Sugar levels should be fine.

Can Food Intolerances Cause Cravings?

There's so much research linking food intolerances with cravings and weight gain, it may be a vital key for you. Food intolerances are more common than food allergies, less severe, and harder to detect. A food allergy is when the immune system reacts to a substance in food, usually a protein, and creates antibodies to fight that "invading" substance. Food allergies can affect multiple organs, whereas food intolerances mostly affect our digestive tract. If you have food allergies you probably know about them, because even the smallest amount can provoke life-threatening reactions. Food allergies can be hereditary.

Food intolerances are a digestive response, rather than an immune response. When we have food intolerances, it's generally because we lack the necessary enzymes to properly digest that food. If an individual is dairy intolerant, that person probably lacks lactase, an enzyme produced in the small intestine needed to breakdown lactose, the disaccharide molecule in dairy. Our bodies' ability to produce lactase often decreases with age. If an individual who is lactose intolerant consumes dairy, he or she may experience digestive disturbances, but not necessarily.

Symptoms of food intolerance can come and go, be mild, and difficult to pinpoint. They vary in their severity and can take anywhere from minutes to days to appear. They can be more severe when you first reintroduce a food into your diet, and lessen as your body adjusts to that food. However, even if your symptoms disappear your body may still be aggravated by that food.

Our bodies' tolerance and symptoms vary. You may get a stuffy nose from eating wheat for example, and then the next time you eat it, you feel fine. That's why food sensitivities can be difficult to detect.

I've experienced times when my body tolerated a food for a while before I noticed symptoms. After taking a break from those foods, I was able to tolerate them again in moderation, but as soon as I'd eat them more frequently, or in larger quantities, I'd become sensitive to them again.

The other thing that's common with food sensitivities is that our bodies develop "immunity" toward certain foods, so we need more and more to feel satisfied. For a couple of years I became addicted to Cocoa. I'd mix a spoon of unsweetened cocoa in hot water with unsweetened almond milk and stevia. At a certain point, I was drinking three to four cups a day and adding more and more Cocoa, because it became less and less satisfying. My body was becoming intolerant to Cocoa, yet my cravings grew stronger. It's odd that we crave the foods to which our bodies are sensitive. I've frequently found that to be true.

I wasn't craving Sugar, which can be the case for Chocolate lovers. My body was reacting to Cocoa, yet I craved more. That's a common indicator of food sensitivities. After eliminating it for several months, I can now enjoy it, without needing more and more to feel satisfied. Some people lose weight when they eliminate their food sensitivities, while eating the same amount of calories. Our body protects itself from irritating foods by holding water and gaining weight. When I binge on foods to which I'm sensitive, like Bread, I get puffy and gain weight overnight.

Eating foods you're intolerant to causes emotional and behavioral imbalances, impacting you in multiple ways. You may think a doughnut is going to make you feel better, but if you're sensitive to wheat and Sugar, as many of us are, after an initial "high", you can get depressed and feel horrible.

Common Food Sensitivities

- Gluten
- Wheat
- Corn
- Dairy
- Soy
- Peanuts
- Eggs
- Nuts
- Shellfish
- Citrus
- Tomato
- Coffee
- Pork
- Chocolate

Symptoms of Food Sensitivities

- Cravings
- Feeling unsatisfied (A strong indicator is when you feel like the more you eat the more you want)
- Headachy
- Water retention, weight gain
- Runny or stuffy nose, itchy eyes, clearing throat
- Canker soars in mouth

- Constipated, gassy, diarrhea, bloated abdomen
- Lethargic, fatigue, difficulty concentrating
- Depressed, moody, agitated, needy, not yourself, emotionally unstable

Discovering Your Food Sensitivities

Have you experienced any of the symptoms listed above? It helps to take notes of what you eat and how you feel afterwards, so that you can begin to identify which foods may be causing your symptoms. If you suspect, or identify a food intolerance, I recommend taking a break from it to see if you feel better, especially if you crave it.

This process is unique for each of us. You may be ready to take a break from certain foods, and there may be other foods to which you're still attached, even though you know they're not right for you. There may be still other foods you're suspicious of, but need to continue eating to determine whether they're aggravating you in some way.

I don't expect you to eliminate anything you're not ready to let go of. This can take time. As you become more attuned to your body, you'll naturally gravitate towards foods that make you feel good, beyond a temporary high.

The best way to observe how foods affect you is to eliminate all the common food allergens for at least two weeks to give your symptoms time to clear. Otherwise, it can be difficult to determine which foods are causing an imbalance. You need a clean slate, particularly if you have multiple intolerances and symptoms.

If you have too many food sensitivities to eliminate at once, I recommend a rotation diet. A rotation diet is when you vary foods, taking a few days break from your suspected food sensitivities each time you consume them. If you can eliminate all the common suspects at once, when you feel better, reintroduce one food at a time. I highly recommend keeping a food journal and recording what you eat and your body's reactions to it, while tracking your mental and emotional states.

Food affects us on multiple levels. Even our outlook on life can change from what we eat. Have you noticed the multifaceted impact food has on you? When I eat Sugar I can't focus. I get agitated, and want more. The negative consequences of not getting work done, because it usually turns into a binge, making me fat and depressed, far outweigh the pleasure.

Your body and mind are intricately connected. What you eat affects your mood, thoughts, and behavior. Your thoughts and emotions affect your body. Certain emotions can make you hungry or lose your appetite in an instant, regardless of whether you just ate. How do your emotions affect your appetite? Do you eat more or less when you're angry, or sad for example? Does it vary depending on the emotion?

If you battle cravings, eliminate your trigger foods and suspect intolerances until your body comes back into balance. If you're interested in identifying your problematic foods through an elimination diet, I recommend working with a nutritionist. It takes planning and support.

I think the biggest challenge in following an elimination diet is our emotions. The hopelessness from failed attempts at healthy eating and weight loss hinders our ability to follow through. My accompanying guided meditations clear your emotions, so that you can connect with why it's important for you to follow an elimination diet, if you choose to do so. Trust your intuition to determine what's right for you.

I'm here to help you. Words can't express my compassion for your struggles and dedication to helping you find freedom and fulfillment, or whatever it is you long for. Fulfilling my destiny has propelled me through numerous challenges. I won't give up on you, and I hope you won't give up on healing yourself either.

The Process of Discovery

Here are a few examples detailing my observations of my suspected food sensitivities to give you an idea of what to look for in yourself. Once you identify the foods that may be causing your symptoms and cravings, you can make smarter choices.

Cheese

I've gone back and forth between eating and eliminating dairy for years. My body is less reactive to raw dairy than pasteurized cow's milk. I was okay with goat dairy for a while, until I compulsively ate large amounts, repeatedly. After taking long breaks from it for months at a time, I can now enjoy small amounts occasionally without any significant symptoms or cravings. In the same way overeating a food can turn it into a trigger food, eating the same foods excessively, or repeatedly can make us sensitive to them, particularly the common food allergens.

Are there foods you eat all the time that you've become attached to? Do you stock up, or go shopping to make sure you never run out of certain items? It's often the foods we eat most that we become sensitive to. I've eliminated dairy for years at a time and then experienced a range of symptoms after eating it again. One time I literally threw up after eating crumbled blue cheese on my salad. That was after eating raw, vegan food for several weeks, so the blue cheese was probably too rich for me at the time. Not a good way to ease out of a detoxifying diet.

Otherwise my reaction to dairy is fairly mild, but disturbing enough to be mindful of when, and how much I eat it. Mostly I get a slightly runny nose, or have to clear my throat repeatedly. I can get gassy, and, or slightly constipated. Even though I love cheese, I buy small quantities as a treat. I pay attention to my symptoms and only eat as much as my body can tolerate, and take long breaks. The quantity and frequency with which you consume your problematic foods usually impacts how well your body tolerates them.

Chocolate

I want to say more about Chocolate even though I already shared my experience with hot cocoa, because many of us have an ongoing relationship with it. I find Chocolate incredibly stimulating. The sensations in my mouth can be so intense and momentarily satisfying it's like the dark, sweet creaminess is making love to my taste buds, giving me bursts of pleasure. I can't think of a food like it.

Chocolate is like a drug, and for many of us a highly addictive one. I always want more. I think it's partly because of my glucose sensitivity and partly because I'm a recovering compulsive eater. But I've noticed that many people eat Chocolate that don't have weight problems. I don't think there's anything wrong with eating Chocolate, unless it makes you suffer. If you always want more, and addictively eat it, perhaps it's not worth the momentary pleasure. Or you may discover you're more of a grazer. You might feel satisfied with one piece, but then an hour or two later you wander back into the kitchen for more. Are you at peace with your

Chocolate consumption, or do you battle cravings, or suffer consequences when you eat it?

It's important to recognize whether you feel satisfied with what you eat. If eating something increases your desire for it, why even begin? If certain foods trigger a battle between Piggy and Watchdog, you may want to consider whether they're worth the struggle. Determining, and being honest with yourself as to which foods trigger a desire for more is liberating. When you eliminate them you may miss them initially, but it's a relief when you stop craving them. Then you can decide whether you want them in your life on a regular basis. Cravings can also come from the mind. When you eat foods you thought you wanted, and feel disappointed, it may have been caused by a memory of how that food tasted in the past. Sometimes your mind is in a habit of desiring something, but when you tune into your body you realize you don't even really want that food.

Find healthy, satisfying treats that make you feel good, so that you can easily maintain your weight. I mostly stay away from Chocolate because I don't want to battle my desire for more. Some of my clients feel more satisfied, and eat less overall when they include dark Chocolate in their healthy eating plan. Some people lose weight, eating butter! Our bodies metabolize and react to foods differently. The intuitive intelligence of your heart enables you to discover what works for your body.

There are several foods that aren't part of my life on a regular basis, including most the trigger foods listed above. I particularly stay away from Sugar, wheat, refined foods, fried foods, and my personal trigger foods.

Which foods are you tired of battling and ready to give yourself a break from?

Mindful Watchdog Activity: Taking a Break From

Trigger Foods

Whether it's Sugar, a food sensitivity, a food from childhood, or a food you've overeaten, taking a break from the foods that trigger you can be pivotal in overcoming cravings.

Journaling or talking with a buddy about symptoms like fatigue, bloating, gas, or intense cravings, to name a few, and brainstorming to figure out which foods might be the culprits, are excellent ways to identify your problematic foods. You can also experiment with recording what you eat, and taking note of how you feel afterwards. After you narrow it down to a few suspects, try eliminating them to see whether there's a difference in your symptoms and cravings, then read what you wrote and notice if there are any trends. Do you crave sweet, fatty, or salty foods? Perhaps your body's asking for more protein, healthy fats, or wholesome carbohydrates. Find healthy alternatives to the foods you crave, by replacing refined foods with whole foods. You can even start with transitional foods. Here's how you'd replace a refined product with a transitional food, until you're ready to switch to a whole food.

If your trigger food are Potato chips, your transitional food could be baked chips, nuts, or roasted Edamames. Baked chips are still processed, but they usually don't contain trans fats and heated oils, so they're a good transitional food. Nuts and Edamames are whole foods, so if you don't have a problem with them, they're good options. Make sure they're not roasted in poor quality oils or trans fats.

Baked Potatoes are an excellent replacement for chips. You could even roast them in the oven with olive oil, salt, and fresh herbs, so that they're nice and crispy. A sweet Potato with Butter, Salt, and a drizzle of Maple syrup can be an excellent way to satisfy a craving for salty and sweet. Once you determine which foods to eliminate think of healthy alternatives, like in the example above, and experiment to find satisfying options.

If you're not ready to let go of your trigger foods, lovingly observe what happens to you when you eat them. Pay attention to how they impact you physically, mentally, and emotionally, and then revaluate your decision based on your insights. You will feel so much better when you discover which foods to avoid, so that your appetite comes into balance, and you lose weight naturally.

Even though it's helpful to identify what triggers your cravings, there are times we just want foods for no particular reason. However, it's incredibly rewarding to be able to choose whether you'd like to eat them, or not.

Satisfying Cravings Summary

Identify your trigger foods, and replace them with transitional, or whole foods, or enjoy them in moderation- if you can. If you end up bingeing, don't buy that food until you feel ready to try it again. Most refined foods simply aren't part of my life on a regular basis, because I'm so much happier without them. In moments of craving, connect with your heart, so that the physical and emotional sensations can lovingly be embraced, and transformed. If it's difficult to feel your emotions, or you prefer to express them: connect with your heart as you playfully act them out. Continue expressing until you feel relaxed, and your cravings subside.

Remember, you don't need to fulfill every craving– they pass on their own. Connect with your heart so that you can discover what you're really needing, and connect with your inner sources of nourishment, or find healthy ways to satisfy your needs. If you struggle with cravings, listen to my *Satisfying Cravings in Healthy, Fulfilling Ways meditation* as much as possible. It will help you make healthy, satisfying choices even when you want to eat comfort foods. It guides you through the process of feeling your desires, letting them pass, and choosing healthy alternatives.

Nutrition Tip: 5 Is it better to drink artificially sweetened diet soda or sugar sweetened regular soda?

There's big money at stake here, and the research seems somewhat biased, contradictory, and inconclusive. Since artificial sweeteners are non-nutritive (don't add calories), some studies suggest that switching from regular, to diet soda can lead to weight loss. Other studies have shown an increase in weight from consuming artificial sweeteners, compared to those consuming a similar overall caloric intake.

Other studies found that people lost more weight drinking diet soda than drinking water, because they reported a decrease in appetite. While other studies suggest artificial sweeteners increase your appetite. In the 70's studies found that artificial sweeteners caused bladder cancer in rats, but when research was done on humans there wasn't enough conclusive evidence. There was speculation that brain tumors were caused by artificial sweeteners, but again the evidence remained inconclusive with too many variables.

It took decades for scientific research to prove the carcinogenic effects of nicotine. It will likely take decades to determine the health implications of cell phone use and wireless Internet, but I find it unavoidable. With a topic as controversial, and with as much inconclusive research as with artificial sweeteners, I would caution you, but as always please make your own decisions and check with your doctor.

The alarming rise in obesity and disease could arguably be linked to the increasing number of artificially man-made substances we consume. I personally only consume food and beverages found in nature. For overall health I encourage people to decrease, or eliminate any kind soda, and replace it with pure water, unsweetened herbal teas, and natural fruit/herbal infused still or sparkling water.

DrMercola.com, How Artificial Sweeteners Confuse your Body into Storing Fat and Inducing Diabetes
http://articles.mercola.com/sites/articles/archive/2014/12/23/artificial-sweeteners-confuse-body.aspx

National Cancer Institute, Artificial Sweeteners and Cancer
http://www.cancer.gov/about-cancer/causes-prevention/risk/diet/artificial-sweeteners-fact-sheet
Mayo Clinic, Artificial Sweeteners and other Sugar Substitutes
http://www.mayoclinic.org/healthy-lifestyle/nutrition-and-healthy-eating/in-depth/artificial-sweeteners/art-20046936?pg=2
WebMD.com, The Diet Soda Debate
http://www.webmd.com/diet/20140731/diet-soda-debate?page=1

Chapter Ten

Stopping When Your Body Has Had Enough

What makes one person able to stop after one bite, and another person unable to access the "enough" button, especially with certain foods? When you're connected to your body, it's easy to receive the signal of fullness and stop when your body's had enough. The less you eat, the less you want, but then why is it so easy to get caught in endless cycles of overeating? Does what you eat matter more than how much you eat? Once an overeater, always an overeater? Can an overeater learn moderation?

Master the art of stopping when your body's had enough, so that you can enjoy food more, and the body you desire.

Cory's Success Story

"After listening to the mediation about over eating, I felt a sense of self acceptance that was missing. I have chronically over eaten for decades and I would commonly feel the emotional weight of shame and criticalness after feeling heavy with food inside. With one experience of Tarika's meditation, I have a new lightness of self-love that has helped me with meal times sense. Simple, powerful, effective.

Thank you Tarika."
Cory Shank, Marin.

This chapter is dedicated to those who find it difficult to stop when your body's had enough. I hold space for each of you in my heart. I know how challenging it can be to stop when you want more, as it's been my greatest challenge.

I imagine everyone on the planet with access to the over-abundance of food that many of us have today, has overeaten at one time or another. The consequences of overeating are most noticeable when it becomes a habit. But even if you don't gain weight from occasionally overeating, you'll feel better the more you respect your signals of fullness. Eating more than your body needs doesn't feel good, does it?

The Divine Eating Experience meditation is vital to stopping when your body's had enough. It enhances your enjoyment of food, so that you feel satisfied, and enables you to receive signals of fullness. If you habitually eat more than your body needs, I highly recommend reviewing that chapter and listening to the Divine Eating Experience meditation as much as possible.

Each chapter helps you establish a convenient, satisfying rhythm of eating, so that it becomes easy to stop when your body's had enough. When you prepare your meals with love, and take time to enjoy eating, you're more likely to feel satisfied. Your choices at the grocery store influence what, and how much you eat. When you're centered in social situations and you ask for what you want, you're more likely to feel good when you're done eating. When you eliminate your trigger foods and satisfy your cravings with whole foods, it's easier to stop when your body's had enough. This entire process prepares you to be able to stop eating when your body's had enough, even when a part of you wants more.

Satisfying Cravings in Healthy Fulfilling Ways is about selecting nourishing foods, or finding healthy ways to fulfill your needs other than eating, whereas now we're focusing on quantities. What you eat, and how much you eat, are equally important. Most people can get away with drinking wine and eating pizza, as long as they eat moderate portions, and not too often. You can be healthy eating large quantities of food, as long as you primarily eat vegetables and salad (without too much dressing), and go easy on concentrated food groups like fats, starches, and proteins.

I mostly choose high-fiber, nutrient dense foods because they're the most satiating, while including small portions of festive foods. I still need to be careful because even in small portions, as part of a balanced meal, the addictive nature of certain foods can make me crave them again the next day. Knowing that enables me to let cravings pass, and wait for a while until I eat those types of foods again.

The Nature of Habits

There are combinations of reasons that drive us to overeat. A habit can begin with a few extra bites because it tastes good, but when we do something repeatedly, the impulses to continue eating become imprinted in our brain and nervous system.

Habits are a combination of physical, psychological, and emotional impulses. These meditations rewire you. They change the neurological and behavioral impulses that drive you to overeat, by expanding your awareness, so that you can make new choices.

259

When you overeat, your body expects larger quantities. When you eat past fullness repeatedly, it becomes a habit making it more and more difficult to stop.

Your emotions and unmet needs can cause you to overeat in the same way they trigger cravings. Overeating and cravings are closely linked. We often overeat the foods we crave because they're addictive. Eating is even more stimulating than fantasizing about food, so the impulses to continue can easily take over. When you overeat you're probably not even in touch with your body, it can sometimes feel as though you're in a trance.

We try to nourish ourselves, and soothe our stresses through food, but emotional hunger is insatiable. When you're eating for reasons other than physical nourishment, the more you eat, the less satisfied you feel, so you just keep eating. Eating can't relieve stress. Feeling, and expressing tension or any other emotional energy, like we did in chapter nine, Satisfying Cravings in Healthy Fulfilling Ways, releases stressful emotions so that you can determine whether you're hungry, what you need, and respond accordingly. Those who struggle with food, often react to hunger in a panic, thinking they're going to starve to death if they don't eat immediately. Those irrational impulses cloud our natural ability to tune into our bodies to determine what we need.

Expressing your emotions can help clear the feelings that make you want to eat, and the disproportionate reactions to hunger, so that you can receive and follow your body's wisdom. You'll be amazed how quickly disturbances pass, when you feel your heart, instead of drowning them out by eating.

You may also experience other kinds of hunger after finishing a reasonable amount of food, because your body needs time to adjust to less food. This adjustment is natural and necessary. These feelings pass as your appetite comes into balance, particularly when you stop eating refined foods. I can't stress this enough. I've noticed an increase in my appetite for breakfast, if I eat refined foods or overeat at dinner the night before! When I eliminate Sugar, alcohol, dairy, and wheat for a few days, my appetite decreases and my cravings subside. Food tastes better, and I crave things like oranges and beetroot, instead of wine, cheese, and Chocolate. I receive clear messages from my body and feel satisfied with less and less food. Try eliminating Sugar, alcohol, dairy and wheat for a week, to see how you feel.

It's best to stop eating as soon as you're not hungry anymore, before you feel full. You may feel like you could eat more, but you don't need to, your body's had enough. Once you get the knack you'll feel more satisfied with less food, and your weight will melt away. I still need to be mindful of this, because even when my body's had enough, there's often a desire for more, which usually takes 10-20 min to subside. If you make stopping before you're full a practice you'll be greatly rewarded. When I'm really still hungry, I have more, until my body "tells" me it's had enough. It usually doesn't take nearly as much food as we think we need, or want, to satisfy our nutritional needs. It's often just a few more veggies, and, or a little more chicken or quinoa, for example.

When I'm still hungry after a meal, or in between, I tune into my body to determine whether it's slight hunger that would pass, or a deeper hunger that would linger all afternoon if I didn't eat more.

You can discover how much food you need to satisfy different levels of hunger by experimenting with eating more when it feels like real hunger, and waiting to see if it passes when you feel relatively satisfied. Sometimes you might really still be hungry, not eat, and become ravenous later, and sometimes you might eat more than you thought you needed. With practice and patience, it will become easier and easier for you to determine how much you need. The balance of macronutrients, and types of foods you eat can have a powerful effect on appetite. Some people's cravings abate with animal protein, whereas others feel most satiated with whole grains, and others do best with a balance of macronutrients. Your intuitive sensitivity, that enables you to determine whether your body's had enough, and your ideal balance of macronutrients, will develop overtime. You'll likely need to experiment with different types and quantities of food, while observing your levels of hunger, until you establish an easy, satisfying rhythm.

Make friends with your body, so that you learn how it communicates with you. Observe what happens when you over, or under-eat. When you're connected to your body while you eat, as in the Divine Eating Experience, your body's messages will become loud and clear. You'll be able to recognize what's causing your desire for more. Is it because the food tastes so good, are you trying to relieve stress, fulfill unmet needs, or are you caught in a habit of overeating? Or does your body really need more food?

I'm particularly careful when my desire for more is from anything other than physical hunger, because I know it can't be satisfied with food. Even though it's challenging, I do my best to feel the craving until it passes without eating more.

Patience

Patience is one of Piggy's essential qualities. It helps you relax while you wait for your brain to register fullness. Patience is vital to stopping when your body's had enough, and during plateaus while you're losing weight. If you're following a weight loss plan and you don't see results right away, you'll become frustrated.

Sometimes you might drop a couple pounds in a day, and then you don't lose anything for several days, or weeks even though you're exercising and eating well. Sometimes you can eat a lot before gaining weight. Patience relieves the pressure we often feel when we're trying to lose weight. It enables us to relax with whatever we're experiencing without running to food to try and change how we feel. I noticed that the more I pressured myself to lose weight, the more I obsessed over food. When I focused on establishing a satisfying rhythm of eating, and accepted whatever weight my body naturally settled at, I relaxed and lost weight.

Patience enables you to enjoy your body as it transforms, which can take time. Successful long-term weight loss generally happens slowly. Patience also enables you to wait to eat until you're physically hungry, which is as vital as letting the desire for more pass when your body's had enough. When you eat when you're not hungry, it's difficult to know when to stop because you didn't need food in the first place. Patience will help you in numerous ways!

Patience Meditation

❖ Take long, deep breaths. Feeling your breath flowing in, and flowing out like gentle waves washing upon the shore, bringing you into the heart of this moment.

❖ Patience is a quality inside, which you can connect with in this very moment. As you connect with it allow it to expand, spreading a gentle atmosphere of peacefulness throughout your body.

❖ Imagine a moment when you're eating more than your body needs. You may know that your body's had enough, but the desire to continue eating is stronger. Feel your body. How does the compulsion to continue eating feel? Do you feel tension in your mouth, shoulders, or somewhere else? What's happening?

❖ Continue taking deep breaths, allowing patience to soothe and melt away tension. Feel each wave of desire being enveloped by the timelessness of your heart, letting the impulses that make you reach for more pass, as you relax more deeply. Settling deep into your center.

What to do When You Can't Stop Eating

When you can't stop eating, see what happens when you allow your desire. I know this may sound scary. At first, when I allowed my desire I ate more, but the peace that resulted from accepting my insatiable hunger instead of fighting it, enabled me to connect with my body and innate wisdom. So, soon I was eating less because instead of restricting myself and wanting everything I denied myself, I realized that eating more wasn't going to make me feel better. I discovered I usually needed something other than food. Acceptance evokes the heart, so that the emotional energy that triggered you, and the guilt and shame that often results from overeating, transforms. When your emotions clear, you naturally become centered in your deeper nature, so it becomes easy to make the right choices.

When you resist your attachment to food, by strengthening Watchdog, it rarely works, at least not for long. That's because Watchdog's trying to control Piggy. Then Piggy indulges in rebellion. It doesn't matter whether you're in the negative expression of Piggy or Watchdog; the key is to accept where you are each moment. Relaxing with where you are connects you to their essence- your inner being. Then it becomes easy to make the right choices and stop when your body's had enough. Have you noticed that when you're predominantly in Piggy, it doesn't matter how hard Watchdog tries to prevent you from overeating, Piggy inevitably wins? When you're in Piggy, embrace it. Let it be. Acceptance transforms Piggy from an insatiable monster into magnetic, loving exuberance.

The beauty is that when you connect with Piggy's essence, you automatically connect to Watchdog's essence as well, which enables you to stop eating when your body's had enough. There's no fight or struggle, you don't see yourself as a problem. You simply know what you need. So when Piggy's raiding the refrigerator, respect yourself, find out what you need. Feel Piggy in your heart, look at that part of yourself compassionately, and listen attentively as Piggy communicates its needs. If a child fell off a swing, or asked you for help with their homework, wouldn't you help? When you can't stop eating Piggy is calling for your attention! If you judged a child as being clumsy, would they feel better and get back on their feet?

You judge yourself every time you overeat! Every spoonful is loaded with guilt and shame. Instead of feeling bad about yourself, be kind and compassionate. Bring love to the moments you can't stop eating, they're golden invitations to become mindful. When you eat chips, or drink a bottle of wine, pay attention to how you feel afterwards, or more importantly the next day, or the next time you get on the scale. While you're eating notice whether you're enjoying the food, and whether it satisfies you. If you feel like your hunger is insatiable, connect with your heart. Ask yourself, "What am I needing right now?" Asking that question will key you into your deeper needs and inner resources, so that you can find ways to fulfill them.

Think of the last time you stopped eating or took care of yourself. What helped you? There are probably plenty of moments you make healthy choices. Value your success! Remembering those moments will connect you with the self-care that inspired those choices, so that it becomes stronger and readily available.

Be generous with yourself and make this a priority. Don't you think you owe this gift to yourself? I significantly changed when I took time to shop, cook, work-out, dance, meditate, eat, take saunas, hot tubs,

long showers, rest, watch movies, go out, learn or try
new hobbies, connect with others, and connect the
nurturing qualities of my heart. What nourishes you?

Enjoying More, Eating Less

When you eat it's important to give yourself permission to enjoy what you're eating, so that you feel satisfied. There may be a voice inside saying, "No Tarika, my problem is that I enjoy food too much!" Listen carefully. I've noticed that when I eat compulsively I hardly taste the food. Watchdog says things like, "You shouldn't eat so much, you should skip your next meal to make up for it, or you'll have to exercise this off later." Then it swings back to Piggy and it says things like, "I deserve to eat! I've been doing so well."

Their voices usually distract us from the pleasure of eating, so we want more and more. We often need to slow down to feel satisfied and receive the signal of fullness. Do Piggy and Watchdog argue while you eat? When you feel guilty about what you're eating, do you feel nourished and satisfied?

Most my clients binge because they under-eat, or are too restrictive with foods like fats and carbs. So for many, the best way to stop when your body's had enough is to eat more of the right kinds of foods, at regular meal times. Until you see that Watchdog's strategies don't work, you'll keep restricting yourself and then overeating, unless you're predominantly in Piggy and you've stopped trying. I swung back and forth, but many people spend the majority of their time on one side.

When Watchdog's in control notice whether those strategies work. Have you successfully maintained your weight long-term by watching what you eat, and monitoring everything that touches your lips, or whatever your strategies are? When you're emotional and hungry and you eat to soothe yourself, notice whether eating really makes you feel better.

Recognizing whether Piggy and Watchdog's strategies are effective in the moment they take over is the first step to changing them. Once you see that what you've been doing hasn't gotten you what you want, you'll naturally find new, more effective ways to satisfy your needs. As you reap the rewards of your changes, you'll build momentum, and soon they'll become your new way of living.

Finishing the Food on Your Plate

Your automatic habits may have originated in childhood as a result of being told to finish the food on your plate. Or perhaps you ate to cope with emotional challenges, and now the habit's ingrained. It may have been passed down from generations. Perhaps your grandmother survived a world war by eating whenever food was available, and now you do the same when there's an over-abundance of food.

Finishing the food on your plate is a common, yet unnecessary habit. A while ago I worked with a woman in Florence, Italy. I suggested she leave two bites of food on her plate every time she ate. She triumphantly emailed me a few days later.

Sharani's Success Story

Hi Tarika,
Today is a great day! I did it! This morning I threw away two spoons of yogurt. I can't believe I did it! I'm still celebrating... he, he, he.
This afternoon I felt an impulse to eat. I recognized it was emotional hunger, and after connecting to loving care, I managed to transform it, just by connecting to my heart. I am so happy!
I love you, I love these meditations, and I love myself for the steps I'm taking!

Thank you for supporting me!

Sharani, Tuscany.

Now Sharani has a choice. If she's full, or doesn't enjoy what she's eating, she can throw the rest away. If you have a habit of finishing the food on your plate, try this!

Mindful Watchdog Activity Throw Two Bites of Food Away

Near the end of your meal, connect with the essence of Watchdog as you triumphantly throw two bites of food away. Even if you can finish your food without overeating, it's helpful to build this strength for when you need it. Each time you throw food away you're exercising your ability to stop eating.

Wouldn't you like to choose whether to finish your food? Don't waste precious calories eating things you don't enjoy!

Feel Your Heart in the Middle of a Binge

There have been times when all I could do in the middle of a binge was give space to what I was feeling. Even though I knew I was hurting myself by overeating, trying to force myself to stop exacerbated my desire for more. That was the moment to feel my heart.

Overeating is Piggy's cry for help, that's when you need love most! Connecting with your heart is essential. Your heart dissolves the emotions that drive you to overeat, and the emotions that result from overeating. Your heart gives you space from self-criticism, so that instead of feeling bad about yourself and eating even more, you connect with your power and wisdom. Your heart gives you space from your ideas about how much, or what you should, or shouldn't eat, so that you can tune into what your body needs. Your heart gives you space from the automatic impulses that drive you to make poor choices, so that you can literally stop a habit in its tracks, mid-bite!

When Watchdog criticizes Piggy for overeating you probably feel bad, which makes you want even more, doesn't it? This conflict creates even more pain, so we cut off from pain, but in doing so we disconnect from our bodies and wisdom because you can't selectively feel. When you're disconnected from your body you can't receive the signal of fullness, so the only way to stop eating is through Watchdog's control, a pre-determined amount.

Unfortunately this exasperates cycles of deprivation and indulgence, fueling the struggle between Piggy and Watchdog. Watchdog eventually forces you to stop, but then Piggy takes over and starts eating again. How many times have you put a bag of chips away and then gone back for more?

Your heart reveals Piggy and Watchdog's essential qualities. Connecting with them is one of the most fulfilling things in life! Your deeper nature gives you the ability to respond to each food situation, and enjoy food without being rigid, while maintaining balance.

Meditation slows down the moment. It's like pausing a movie, or watching yourself eat in slow motion. This gives you distance from the driving impulses of your habits, so that you can connect with what's important to you, consider the consequences of your options, and make empowering choices. At first you may only become aware after you've overeaten. The next time you might become aware of Piggy while you're eating. As you bring awareness to your habits, you'll recognize that the consequences of overeating are uncomfortable, and food can't satisfy your deeper needs. Soon you'll recognize that food isn't going to give you what you want, before you take that first unhealthy bite.

Our problem is that we often ignore and blind ourselves to the consequences of overeating, because hurting ourselves with food is painful. Your heart enables you to see yourself with compassion, so that you can recognize the consequences of your choices without judgment. When you see how foods and quantities affect you before you eat them, you'll naturally select yummy nourishment.

At times you may need to lovingly say, "No." to Piggy, just like a loving parent would say no to their child asking for a lollypop before dinner. And yet, saying, "No." without connecting to your heart usually begins the typical battle between Piggy and Watchdog. Your heart opens the door to your inner sources of love and strength- the essence of Piggy and Watchdog. Saying no to food, when you need to, can be the most caring thing you could possibly do. Each time you care for yourself, you become stronger, and the desire for stimulating foods that leave you empty and unsatisfied, slowly diminishes. The balance shifts, so that healthy foods become more alluring than foods that only "promise" temporary satisfaction.

Forgiveness

I used to feel terrible about myself every time I binged. I'd want to crawl out of my skin. I'll never forget something my mother said to me in a forgiveness meditation.

"If you could have stopped you would have, but you weren't strong enough, and that's okay. It never helps to beat yourself up. Simply acknowledge that you were unaware and forgive yourself." If you can't stop eating, use it as an opportunity to discover what's triggering your desire. Take a deep breath and feel your heart. You can ask your heart to reveal what triggered you. Was it something you ate? Did someone say something that upset you? Was an emotion or unmet need driving your desire for more?

As you eat, feel your body, and notice whether you're enjoying the food. Is it making you feel better, or do you still feel emotional or needy regardless of how much you eat? Allow your heart to embrace the feelings that arise when you're overeating. There may be feelings of hopelessness, a sense of failure, or range of emotions. As your emotions clear, you'll naturally come in touch with the inner strengths that enable you to stop eating. Your heart will reveal more fulfilling ways to respond to your needs.

Don't worry if you're not strong enough to stop the next time you overeat, forgive yourself again. It takes practice and patience. Forgive yourself every time Piggy takes over and eats something that isn't right for you. Forgiveness connects you to infinite sources of unconditional love and compassion, deep within your heart.

Forgiveness Meditation Instructions

This meditation guides you through the process of forgiveness, which was one of the most powerful processes I did. Forgiving myself for eating compulsively and then depriving myself to make up for it, released tremendous guilt and shame.

Forgiveness enables you to let go of past hurts, which accumulate each time you feel bad about yourself, or regret eating. It enables you to come into the moment, so that you don't get taken over by emotions and mindsets that trigger compulsion. Forgiveness prevents hopelessness from spiraling into vicious cycles of unhealthy habits.

Have you noticed that once you start overeating it becomes harder and harder to stop? That's because we feel exponentially powerless each time we get taken over by old habits and ignore signals of hunger and fullness. When you forgive yourself, and realize that your past doesn't need to influence your choices, you feel lighter. Each moment is fresh– a new opportunity to care for yourself.

Forgiveness Meditation

I recommend reading these instructions a couple times and then setting a stopwatch for ten minutes, so that you're not concerned with time. You can do this meditation as often as you like, especially after overeating.

❖ Find a comfortable position, preferably in front of a mirror.
❖ Take a deep breath and close your eyes for few moments to connect with your heart. Feel the soothing atmosphere of your heart surrounding you with love.
❖ Open your eyes and look into the mirror and say to yourself, (your name) I forgive you for eating a bag of chips last night. Then forgive yourself for something else, (your name) I forgive you for eating ice cream after you already had wine and ravioli. Or you can ask for forgiveness, (your name or someone else) can you forgive me for eating a bagel the other day?
❖ Say whatever comes to you, allowing it flow from your heart. Forgive yourself for anything you're holding onto, or forgive others that you hold grudges towards, by saying their name instead of yours. If you run out of things to say, repeat the incidences you haven't totally forgiven yourself for. More will come the longer you do this. Keep on forgiving yourself,

and others until you feel the quality of forgiveness in your heart, and you feel lighter.

❖ Then take a deep breath and close your eyes again. Notice how it feels to give and receive forgiveness. Deeply acknowledge and treasure your ability to forgive yourself, and others.

Forgiveness Enables You to Make a Healthy Choice at Your Next Meal

Don't worry if you don't notice the affects of forgiveness right away, or if you can't completely forgive yourself for your lapses of self-love. Even if you forgive a little bit, that's wonderful! Your ability to forgive will grow the more you practice. Forgiving yourself for overeating enables you to make healthier choices instantly, instead of letting your mistakes spiral into bingeing.

Pick Yourself Up, Dust Yourself Off

Remember healing your relationship with food is a journey. You may always need to be conscious of what, and how much you eat. Picking yourself up after unhealthy eating is vital!

You're bound to fall into old habits and make poor choices at times. Don't let them spiral into addictive eating. Forgive yourself and find ways to get back on track instantly! When you have a night of indulgence, make a healthy choice for breakfast.

I've found it's best to get back to your rhythm right away instead of trying to make up for your mistakes by eating less. If you skip breakfast you'll likely get hungry later, which often sets you up to overeat again. You can eat slightly less, or a little later if you're still full from a night of indulgence. Sometimes overeating can make you hungrier. If that's the case, I recommend eating the amount on your food plan, or filling up on high-fiber foods, until your appetite stabilizes. Any type of green vegetable (raw or cooked), protein, and a moderate amount of fat, cuts cravings, and makes me feel better almost instantly. Exercise is extremely beneficial as well.

I fell back into destructive habits so many times, I could have easily given up and gained sixty pounds. But I didn't. I learned to forgive myself, so that I made healthy choices at my next meal.

It's helpful to find things that support you, and commit to doing them regularly, whether you feel like it or not. I exercise 5 times a week regardless of how I feel. It's become a habit and it always makes me feel better. Another supportive habit is drinking green juice. Do I feel like drinking it, or exercising after a night of festivity? Hardly ever, but I do it anyway because it makes me feel good, and keeps me on track.

When I don't care for myself, I indulge again the next night. If I miss another opportunity to eat well, or exercise, I continue to indulge until I come back to protein and vegetables, so why wait? When I'm traveling, or eating out I make the healthiest choices possible. Your intuitive intelligence will find healthy, creative solutions, so that you can do the best you can, wherever you are. Find ways to care for yourself and turn them into healthy routines, so that it becomes effortless.

Mindfulness isn't Linear. Transformation is Circular.

You may be doing very well for a while, maintaining your weight, enjoying your life and food, and then all of the sudden you fall back into the same old habits. It's common to take one step forward and two steps back at times, especially when you've struggled long-term.

You may get caught in hopelessness thinking you're never going to change. Negative mindsets can blind you from being able to recognize and value your progress. If you're thinking, "I should be beyond this by now!" then you'll feel like a failure when you fall back into old habits. I promise you, even though it may not seem like you're making progress in those moments, you are changing. You might have a little more space from the habit. There's probably a longer gap before your habits take over. Maybe in the past you became mindful of your habits after you overate, and perhaps now you're aware of your impulses before you begin eating. You may sense that you have a choice. Even though you may not always be strong enough to make another choice, becoming mindful while you're overeating, or before you begin eating, is a major improvement!

Even if you're just a little more accepting of yourself, and feel compassion for the part that wants food more than anything, that's wonderful. Your emotional reaction to your unconscious food choices may be different. When you're not condemning yourself you may be able to see yourself in a new light, and have a greater understanding of your triggers and needs.

As your meditation deepens and you become more centered in food situations, there are often periods when you don't see results for a while. It's vital for you to acknowledge the little changes in how you perceive yourself, life, and others. As you value them they'll grow, and in time you'll be strong enough to make empowering choices before your habits take over. You'll be able to feel your desires, see where your unhealthy habits lead, and not even go there.

I want to share a story with you to illustrate this to make sure you keep going until you're successful. Don't give up when you fall back into old habits! Always remember, if you accidently eat foods that aren't right for you, you're not a failure. Simply forgive yourself for your mistake, and make a healthy choice at your next meal. It was around 10:00 p.m., my usual time to binge, especially after spending long days at the spa taking care of others. I felt depleted, yet wired and discontented. I needed "something." My fridge called out to me. I took a deep breath and felt my heart. I tried to unwind with a movie, but I kept thinking about food. I tried to feel my heart again, but this time my cravings took over. I needed food now! I started with a warm, grain beverage, but I wasn't satisfied. I opened the refrigerator, but I was trying to lose weight, so there weren't any comfort foods.

After rummaging through the cupboards I found some millet, which I ground into flour and made a crepe. I stuffed it down quickly, eating with my fingers over the stove. I stopped. What on earth was I doing? I was determined to find freedom, and here I was overeating again. I had seen this episode so many times. I ate another crepe, but I still wasn't satisfied. I felt lonely and hopeless– like I was never going to change. I made another one and ate it frantically, hoping to soothe my guilt and shame, but I didn't feel any better. After the fourth crepe I realized my hunger was insatiable. I wasn't even physically hungry! I needed love and attention. Crepes, or any food, would never satisfy my longing for intimacy. Eating was actually making me feel worse about myself.

The next morning I woke up to another dreary, foggy day in Mill Valley. I made a cup of tea, but since I felt "hung over" from last night's binge, I decided to go back to bed. I sobbed for twenty minutes. How could I betray myself yet again, after all I had been through? I turned over and looked into the mirror across from my bed. I felt another wave of tears and self-condemnation. Why was it so difficult to change?

As I continued to look at myself, I connected with my forgiving heart. As I forgave myself I was filled with compassion. After another brief release of tears I began to embrace my reflection. As I lovingly looked at myself, I noticed my perception of my body was clearing. Even though I was heavier than where I felt comfortable, I felt more at peace. As I began to accept myself I felt a quality of love spread through my whole body, embracing the parts I despised.

I no longer feared Piggy, who had been my darkest demon. I was beginning to see my beauty and strength. I stopped judging my insatiable monster. I saw that eating was Piggy's attempt to care for me. Piggy's essence is loving, joyful, juicy, dynamic, intuitive, and magnetic. Piggy gave me my gifts as a healer, partner, and friend.

I went to my whiteboard in the kitchen and started writing. I came up with several questions, which I used every morning after I binged.

- What can I learn from this experience?
- What's the most caring thing I can do for myself today?
- How can I satisfy my needs in ways other than eating the next time I have a craving?
- Did a particular food, person, situation, or unmet need trigger Piggy's compulsion?

Forgiveness is one of the biggest keys for healing your relationship with food. You're bound to eat things that aren't right for you. Instead of beating yourself up and falling into a downward spiral, connect with compassion and forgive yourself. Then use it as an opportunity to learn from your lapse of self-love by asking these, or your own version of similar questions.

That day I was particularly loving and gentle with myself. I didn't punish myself by not eating, or force myself to work out. I ate light, went for a walk, and drank herbal teas and lots of water. I decided to show up for myself, even though there wasn't a man in my life. I did the things I longed to do, instead of waiting at home alone for someone to share my life with.

I continued to fall back into unhealthy habits for a while, but I learned to pick myself up quickly, instead of spiraling into addictive eating. I called this phase "bringing love to bingeing." When I wasn't strong enough to stop eating I went with it. Instead of rejecting Piggy, which made me want to eat more, I embraced that part of me. As I welcomed Piggy into my heart I discovered, and connected with what I was really longing for, which was mostly love and care.

As I stopped judging myself I became aware of how overeating affected me physically and emotionally, and that it didn't satisfy my needs. So overeating became less and less appealing, and eventually futile in the same way my weight loss strategies lost their grip over me.

I was finally becoming free! I stopped dieting. My obsessive exercise habits turned into playful, engaging, yet sufficiently challenging forms of movement. My binges became less and less frequent, in smaller quantities, and healthier, nutritionally balanced foods. Sure, sometimes I ate a little more than by body needed, like many people do on occasion, but then I'd eat less to maintain balance. I didn't skip meals or over-exercise to make up for it.

Reasons for Change

Don't let fashion models; celebrities, or advertisers on TV determine how you should look! Ask yourself, "What makes me feel comfortable and beautiful?" What will eating healthily give me?" The most powerful reasons for change are those that benefit you! Connecting with what's important to you carries you through the challenges of healthy eating. It connects you to your deeper nature- your true power.

When I wanted to lose weight but couldn't stop eating, I questioned my motivation. I blamed my habits on my schedule, the fact that I didn't have a boyfriend, and stress. In the past, I lost weight to become more attractive to men, and to avoid the embarrassment of squeezing into my jeans. Fortunately, those reasons weren't strong enough anymore. I didn't care about men as much at the time, or what others thought, and I stopped wearing jeans. I didn't go to the other extreme and gain more weight. I took care of myself as best as I could, and started to appreciate my body the way it was. I certainly would have preferred to be lighter, but I couldn't lose weight at the time.

I needed to accept my body regardless of what I weighed. I was ready to break free from the need to be skinny in order to feel beautiful. I didn't want my self-worth to be tied to how much I weighed. After releasing the pressure caused by society's beauty standards, I realized I simply felt better when I was lighter. Getting in touch with why it was important for me to break my destructive habits enabled me to make the changes necessary to achieve what I longed for.

Feeling good physically, mentally, and emotionally became more important than popcorn, or whatever food I was craving. At the time I was fixated on popcorn. I saw how destructive eating popcorn was. Each time I wanted popcorn I considered whether it was worth the suffering. I occasionally went with the desire, but soon feeling good became stronger.

I'd think about the weight I'd gain and how uncomfortable it would make me feel. I'd remember the pain and hopelessness I felt every time I binged, and the agony of dieting. This may sound obvious, but most of us ignore these consequences when we're craving. Since

I've become mindful of how certain foods affect me, I know what to expect and in many cases I just don't eat them anymore. When I lost weight to become more attractive to my boyfriend, I'd gain it back as soon as we split up, because I was losing weight for him.

If you're trying to change because of your doctor, even if you need to for your health, it's still important to connect with why becoming healthier is important to you. Valuing the results of healthy eating, enables you to choose wisely and stop even when you want more.

Reasons for Change Meditation

To help you feel your body and come into the moment, shake out your hands, or other parts of your body. Take a deep breath, letting go of any stress or tension as you breath out.

- ❖ Now imagine yourself five years from now, and nothing's changed. See yourself getting fatter, or starving yourself, still battling Piggy and Watchdog. Feel what the affects will be if you continue to eat in these ways. Perhaps you need bigger clothes, maybe your partner isn't as attracted to you, or your job is in jeopardy. Imagine, and feel what your future will be like if you continue to eat this way.
- ❖ Imagine what will happen ten years from now if you keep gaining weight. Maybe your health is deteriorating; because no matter how hard you try, you can't stop eating.
- ❖ Take another deep breath, and imagine yourself stepping back into the present. Shake off the past by shaking your body again.

Connect with why it's important for you to change. When you looked into the future, what weren't you doing that's important to you? Perhaps you weren't vital enough to play with your kids, or you didn't accomplish your life's purpose because you wasted your time eating.

❖ Take another deep breath and feel your heart. Connect with what you really want in your life, and feel what that would give you. Feel the energy of it fill your whole body. See yourself looking vibrant and beautiful, taking care of your body. Value yourself for the changes you're already making, and for taking time to read this book.

Mindful Watchdog Activity Reasons for Change Journaling

You can write about your experience during the meditation, or answer these questions instead, or in addition to the meditation. Write about what's important to you. How will your life be different if you eat the right types, and quantities of food for your body? How will you feel, and what can you accomplish by taking care of yourself? Keep writing until you uncover compelling reasons to eat healthily. At first you may list superficial reasons, like the way you want others to see you. If you continue you'll come to deeper, more powerful reasons, and you'll feel it. You may hear yourself sigh with relief or your heart might flutter with excitement as you discover what's true for you.

Connecting to What's Important to You

Once you uncover meaningful reasons to change it's important to connect with them regularly. Every time you want to continue eating after you've had enough, connect with how good you'll feel if you stop before you're uncomfortably full. When you feel left out as you watch others eat ice cream, connect with how you want to feel. Consider the consequences of eating ice cream; through your heart, to see whether it will give you what you want.

When you plateau in your weight or fall back into unhealthy habits, connect with why it's important for you to take better care of yourself. Connect with your reasons to change each time you feel challenged to make a healthy choice.

Change Happens In the Moment

I used to think there was something to achieve. I thought if I ate perfectly and maintained my "perfect" weight, I'd be happy. Since then I've realized that finding a peaceful, balanced relationship with my body and food is a journey. Breaking habits happens in the moment. I've never found a "perfect weight" or way of eating. It's always changing based on what I need each moment.

You change by making healthy choices each time you have an impulse to eat things that aren't right for you, and by stopping when your body's had enough. Have you ever changed by making a commitment to start a diet "tomorrow"? "Tomorrow" often takes weeks, months, or years to come, doesn't it? Secondly, at this point you probably realize that dieting doesn't work long-term, unless your new way of eating becomes a lifestyle. Dieting usually leads to all-or-nothing. "All" is Watchdog trying to eat perfectly, and "nothing" is Piggy eating whatever it wants.

Your heart enables you to choose what's right for you each moment, beyond the extremes of "all" or "nothing". One moment Piggy might eat a brownie, and the next moment Watchdog might engage in a fun activity. It becomes a beautiful dance that naturally brings you into balance.

I wish I could get rid of your habits, or prescribe the perfect food plan to miraculously transform your body. Unfortunately, I haven't found a magic pill. You'll change by making one empowering choice at a time. It can be challenging, because we need to make multiple food choices daily. You might make healthy choices 70% of the time, which is excellent! Unfortunately, 30% of mindless eating can impair your healthy choices, depending on your situation. That's one of the reasons we can feel like a failure even when we're actually making excellent progress.

When you feel like your doing well, but aren't getting results, do you give up and eat whatever you want? Or does Watchdog try to enforce stricter rules, thinking you haven't found the right strategy? Sometimes we need to make healthy choices 90% of time, at least initially, to get results. To increase the percentage, continually learn from your mistakes and focus on your success. Whatever you focus on grows. Don't obsess over slipups, learn from them and move on. Bring attention to, and value the healthy choices you make because they will grow exponentially.

Better Than

"Better Than" breaks the all-or-nothing syndrome. Have you "failed" at a diet because of perfectionism? Better Than enables you to make the best choice possible each moment. Even when your choices aren't perfect, they might be Better Than what you'd normally eat. Wheatgrass is best drunken on an empty stomach immediately after juicing, but because of my habits and schedule, I couldn't find the "right time" to drink it. My precious wheatgrass often went to waste.

I experimented with Better Than and drank it whenever I could. Sometimes I drank it thirty minutes after my black tea. A couple times I drank it after a decaf coffee with soymilk, which I don't recommend, but it helped me establish a rhythm. Sometimes I only waited twenty minutes, instead of ninety minutes, after drinking it before my breakfast smoothie. To Watchdog that was unacceptable! Wheatgrass was hard enough to integrate into my life without setting myself up to fail by being rigid. Over time I established a routine.

Better Than enables you to make changes based on where you are. It will naturally increase the percentage of your healthy choices. If you wait until you can make perfect choices all the time, you might never change! Have you come across anyone who's "perfect"?

I used to struggle with the all-or-nothing syndrome with exercise as well. If I didn't have at least ninety minutes, I skipped my workout, but then I wouldn't feel as good. I decided to experiment. When I woke up late, or had early appointments I did what I could. I always felt better afterwards. Better Than continues to help me in numerous ways, including, and beyond, how I care for my body. How can Better Than help you? What do you give up on when you can't make perfect choices?

Better Than—Balance Between Piggy and Watchdog

I encourage you to develop this skill. It will help you in more ways than you can imagine! You may like to write about the situations in which you give up on eating healthy, when you don't see any satisfying options.

Do you eat a hamburger at a fast food restaurant because the chicken salad isn't organic? Do you eat a scone with your coffee, because you think the fruit salad is too high in Sugar? I know it sounds absurd, but have you ever done things like that? I used to. Many do! Think of one or two situations that happen regularly to

291

practice making Better Than choices. As you improve, take time to appreciate your progress, by valuing the little, and big changes you make.

Watchdog's clarity enables you to determine which Better Than choices to make. For example, maybe you want to switch from half and half to low fat milk or perhaps you're not ready to let go of Chocolate, but you can replace Milk Chocolate with organic 85% Dark Chocolate. You'll find many opportunities to make Better Than choices. Better Than has a powerful snowball effect. Your choices will get better and better, giving you better and better results.

Reward Yourself As You Lose Weight!

Most people think they need to lose weight before they deserve to celebrate. You may want to try giving yourself gifts to acknowledge your efforts along the way. Rewarding yourself in ways other than eating keeps you inspired, in spite of your successes and failures.

Acknowledge yourself and value your progress every step of the way. Treat yourself to a massage, hire a trainer, take a vacation, or buy new clothes, so that you feel comfortable and beautiful, as you lose weight.

Enjoy the journey. Enjoy your curves. Perhaps your breasts are more beautiful when you're heavier, or maybe you feel stronger. Love and appreciate your body as it is right now! Your heart makes this possible! You may not attract every man, but there are plenty of men who desire juicy, round women! Men aren't nearly as critical or picky about the way we look, as we are about ourselves. Radiate Piggy's luscious feminine beauty, and you'll likely be delighted by what you attract.

Above all, please be kind, compassionate, and patient with yourself. Some days will be easier than others. On days you feel more compelled, emotional, or have stronger cravings, listen to these meditations. They'll connect you with your essential qualities, which are nourishing and fulfilling. They'll make it easier for you to make food choices that make you feel good, or find other ways to meet your needs.

You're not alone—just like many others, you can use the power of meditation and the grace of your heart to break unhealthy habits, and reclaim your self-dignity.

Stopping When Your Body Has Had Enough

Summary

Choose highly nutritious foods with the optimal balance of macronutrients for your biochemical individuality, so that you feel more satisfied with less food. Reduce or eliminate refined, processed foods, and be careful when you eat your trigger foods because once you start it can be difficult to stop. Break the habit of finishing the food on your plate with the Throw Two Bites of Food Away Watchdog Mindfulness to develop this strength for when you need it.

When you can't stop eating, bring love to Piggy to discover what you really need. Use it as an opportunity to become more mindful, so that you can discover what's triggering you. Connect with your inner quality of patience as you wait for your brain to register the signal of fullness. Eating more of the right kinds of foods at regular meal times is a far more effective way to lose weight than depriving yourself and under-eating.

If you'd like Tarika to personally coach you on Skype to help you break habits of overeating, like finishing the food on your plate or bingeing, send an email to Tarika@TarikaLovegarden.com

Nutrition Tip: 6 Do the types of carbohydrates make a difference in terms of satiety and weight?

Research has shown that if you consume the same amount of calories, the types of carbohydrates you eat (simple vs. complex) won't effect your body composition (lean body mass, and body fat), provided all else is equal in terms of protein, fat, and overall calories.

However, simple, refined carbs (sweets, white bread, white rice, etc.) will spike your blood sugar levels and won't satisfy your hunger for as long as complex carbohydrates (vegetables, fruit, whole grains), making most people consume more calories, which can lead to weight gain due to the increase in calories. In general the more fiber and water a carbohydrate contains the better for satiety. You'll feel fuller for longer.

A Calorie Counter, Simple vs. Complex, Low Glycemic vs. High Glycemic, Bad vs. Good

http://www.acaloriecounter.com/diet/carbs-simple-complex-high-low-glycemic-good-bad/

Conclusion

Keep it Simple, A Summary Bringing It All Together

Your Kitchen Is Your Sanctuary

Make this easy for yourself! Clean out your fridge and pantry regularly, and throw out, or give away your trigger foods, so that they don't tempt you. If you live with others, particularly kids, find creative ways to separate their foods from yours. One of my clients has a special drawer in the kitchen for her daughter's cookies. If you're the type that can't stop after one, make a firm decision not to go there.

You may want to decorate your fridge with inspiring pictures or magnets that remind you of health and beauty. Play music, watch your favorite shows, or listen to inspirational podcasts and Ted Talks while you cook. Listen to the Cooking with Love meditation, to transform cooking from a chore into a mindful, fun and creative activity. Infuse your food with love, so that your meals are nourishing and flavorful. Experiment with new recipes or create your own.

This is Piggy's playground

Let Piggy run wild and lick the spoon, if you like. Plan and prepare your meals, so that you always have healthy food available for when you, or your family gets hungry.

296

Before You Shop

Connect with your body intuition before you shop. Make a grocery list and tune into the items that might trigger unhealthy eating. Determine whether you're centered enough to buy them, and how much you'll buy before you go into the store. Find healthy, satisfying treats and only buy what you need. Don't buy foods that leave you unsatisfied and wanting more.

Smart Choices at the Grocery Store is the most effective way to connect with your body intuition, so that you can easily determine what you need, moment to moment. Put one or two items back while standing in the checkout line, to break the habit of stocking up, and so that you don't buy items you're likely to overeat. If you accidently buy trigger foods and find yourself eating them on your way home, remember, it's never too late to throw the rest away!

Say Your Prayer

Before you eat, take a deep breath and connect with your heart. Say your Prayer of Grace before you begin eating. Set your worries and concerns aside, so that you can receive nourishment from the foods you eat. Appreciate the shapes and colors on your plate, like you would a beautiful bouquet of roses. Smelling your food can awaken and engage your senses, and connect you with your body wisdom. If you generally eat with family, friends, or colleagues, slip away for 2 minutes to center yourself before you begin eating.

Enjoy Eating

Take time to savor each bite, enjoying the different tastes and textures. Mindfully chew each bite, so that you feel satisfied. Let your body guide your fork, so that you receive your signals of fullness, and can stop eating when your body's had enough. You may like to enhance your eating experience with candles, the Divine Eating Experience meditation, or special dishes. Make each meal a delightful, sacred time of nourishment. Enjoy each meal as if it's your first!

Balancing Your Body Nutritionally

Eat whole, unprocessed foods whenever possible. Find the right balance of macronutrients for your body, so that you feel energized and satisfied. Experiment to find your ideal breakfast. Try to include protein, fiber, healthy fats, an abundance of greens, and nourishing carbohydrates with your meals. Focus on foods that satiate, rather than stimulate your appetite. Journal and experiment with eliminating suspect food sensitivities. Drink plenty of water. Find fun activities to move your body, and soothing ways to relax and rejuvenate.

Take a Break from Trigger Foods

Let your appetite come into balance. Satisfy your cravings with whole foods, and connect with your heart, so that the impulses that trigger poor choices pass before you act on them. Remember, you'll crave the foods you eat until you stop eating them. To help you make healthy choices in moments of cravings, listen to the Satisfying

Cravings in Healthy, Fulfilling Ways meditation until it becomes easy to choose foods that satisfy you without negative consequences.

Refuse Food Gifts

If you don't feel good about eating something, politely decline food gifts. You can also graciously receive the gift, and give it to someone else as soon as possible. Make sure you determine whether you'll be tempted to eat it before you have time to give it away. When in doubt throw it out!

If You Binge

Forgive yourself, learn from your mistake, and choose your next meal wisely. Throw the rest of the food away. DON'T save it for later! Be gentle, and treat yourself with extra care, so that you get back to healthy eating as quick as you can.

If You Can't Stop Eating

Bring love to the old habit. Take the opportunity to discover what Piggy is really wanting, other than food. Don't beat yourself up. Piggy needs your love and attention. If you can't stop eating, choose high-fiber, water-rich, whole foods and protein, as much as possible. The Stopping When Your Body's Had Enough audio meditation is excellent for breaking habits of overeating.

When You Go Out

Tune in to your body before you go out to determine what you need. You may want to decide whether you'll have drinks, appetizers, and, or dessert. Connect with Watchdog's essential qualities to ask for what you want. Connect with Piggy's essential qualities, so that you can connect with others, while taking care of your needs. Don't be afraid to leave food on your plate, or take leftovers home for another delicious meal. If this is particularly challenging for you, listen to Eating Healthily in Social Situations, so that you can learn to be centered, enjoy connecting, and feel great the next day.

Your heart is always present, no matter what you're experiencing

Your heart won't abandon you. It never goes away. When you have negative feelings, you tend to focus on the feelings, and forget about the heart. When you say YES to what you're experiencing, your heart naturally opens, giving you the strength and sensitivity to make the right choices. Make healthy choices because it feels good. Remember it's a journey. You are love, and you are lovable. You're already beautiful the way you are, and you will become more beautiful with each healthy choice you make.

I'm here to help you. May your heart be with you.

– Tarika

Made in the USA
Monee, IL
02 October 2023

43814784R10168